Praise for *The Myths of Innovation*

Since its initial publication, The Myths of Innovation *has been discussed at or on NPR, MSNBC, CNBC, Yale University, MIT, Carnegie Mellon University, Microsoft, Apple, Intel, Google, Amazon.com, as well as other major media, corporations, and universities around the world.*

"The naked truth about innovation is ugly, funny, and eye-opening—but it sure isn't what most of us have come to believe. With this book, Berkun sets us free to try to change the world unencumbered with misconceptions about how innovation happens."

> —*Guy Kawasaki, author of* The Art of the Start *and* Rules for Revolutionaries

"Brimming with insights and historical examples, Berkun's book not only debunks widely held myths about innovation, it also points the ways toward making your new ideas stick. Even in today's ultra-busy commercial world, reading this book will be time well spent."

> —*Tom Kelley, GM, IDEO; author of* The Ten Faces of Innovation

"No word in the current business arena is more used with incorrect applicability than the word innovation. Scott's tome is understandable, thoughtful, often contrarian, and a great read."

> —*Richard Saul Wurman, author of* Information Anxiety; creator of the TED conference

"Berkun unravels the misconceptions of where ideas come from with wit, realism, and authority. This book will change the way you think about invention—permanently."

> —*Lifehacker.com*

"It's an easy read that is hard to put down. What's more it's really motivating. After reading this book you will want to dig right back into those crazy ideas."

> —*Slashdot.org*

"It's an entertaining and

> —*London Book R*

"A book that belongs on the same shelf with Thomas Kuhn, Howard Gardner, and Eric Von Hippel, *The Myths of Innovation* will challenge your assumptions about the roots of breakthrough ideas, and inspire you to come up with a few of your own."

—Steven Johnson, author of The Ghost Map and
Everything Bad Is Good For You

"The *Myths of Innovation* is insightful, inspiring, evocative, and just plain fun to read. And on top of that, it goes to the heart of innovation and its many challenges. It's totally great."

—John Seely Brown, Former Director, Xerox Palo Alto
Research Center (PARC)

"Would-be trailblazers and worldchangers should stop waiting for lightning to strike their laptops and study the wisdom Scott Berkun has gathered instead. Methodically and entertainingly dismantling the cliches that surround the process of innovation, Berkun reminds us that there are no shortcuts to breakthroughs—and that creativity is its own reward."

—Scott Rosenberg, author of Dreaming in Code;
cofounder of Salon.com

"I love this book! Wise, witty, packed with fascinating history, compelling anecdotes, and priceless ideas"

—Richard Farson, President, Western Behavioral Sciences
Institute; author of Management of the Absurd:
Paradoxes in Leadership

"Most of what business schools teach about innovation qualifies as urban legend. This book is the remedy: a fun, smart tour of the entrepreneurial spirit, in myth and reality."

—William Poundstone, author of How Would You Move
Mount Fuji?

"Will inspire you to come up with breakthrough ideas of your own."

—Alan Cooper, father of Visual Basic and author of
The Inmates Are Running the Asylum

"How I ran a startup without reading this book baffles the mind."

—Richard Stoakley, CEO, Overcast Media, Inc.

"If you care about being innovative, whether for yourself, your company, or your students, you need to know where the truth lies—what the myths are.

Scott Berkun's book dispels the myths while providing solid advice about the practice. All this in an eminently readable, enjoyable style that delights as it informs. Small, simple, powerful: an innovative book about innovation."

—*Don Norman, Nielsen Norman Group; author of*
Emotional Design *and* The Design of Everyday Things

"This book cuts through the hype, analyzes what is essential, and more importantly, what is not. You will leave with a thorough understanding of what really drives innovation."

—*Werner Vogels, CTO, Amazon.com*

"This book shatters the sacred cows of innovation myths and gives real-world innovators insight into making innovations that matter."

—*Jim Fruchterman, CEO, Benetech; 2006 MacArthur Fellow*

"Berkun shows us what innovation isn't, challenging our preconceived notions of what innovation means. Whether you agree or disagree with Scott, this book will make you think."

—*Gary William Flake, PhD, Founding Director,*
Microsoft Live Labs

"Mythology: innocent storytelling or damaging lies? Berkun looks into innovation myths and reveals how they can damage true organizational creativity. He reveals the myths but also provides an incredibly useful framework for going forward—this is an awesome book."

—*Tara Hunt, Founder, Citizen Agency*

"'The most useful way to think of epiphany is as an occasional bonus of working on tough problems,' explains Berkun in his book, *The Myths of Innovation*."

—*Janet Rae-Dupree,* The New York Times

"*The Myths of Innovation* is not just funny, perceptive, and useful—it's downright inspiring!"

—*Erin McKean, Editor,* Oxford American Dictionary

"A touching intimacy marks Berkun's look at the stories we weave around our technologies...anyone frustrated by the public's fear of new ideas will learn how far more subtle than its mythologies the creative process really is."

—*John H. Lienhard, author of* How Invention Begins; *voice of National Public Radio's* The Engines of Our Ingenuity

"As individuals, corporations, and nations struggle to master the increasing technological and social complexities of the modern world, a deeper understanding of the mechanisms of innovation is required to make effective policy and business decisions. Berkun's approachable and fast-paced book provides an excellent introduction to the issues involved while demolishing common misconceptions and leaving the reader hungry to learn more."

—*Cory Ondrejka, CTO, Linden Lab, creators of* Second Life

"A quick and engaging read. Exposes the realities faced by successful inventors, debunks silver-bullet solutions others wish were true, and offers real approaches for making things that transform our lives."

—*Bo Begole, Manager, Ubiquitous Computing Lab, PARC Research*

"I loved this book. It's an easy-to-read playbook for those wanting to lead and manage positive change in their business."

—*Frank McDermott, Marketing Manager, EMI Music*

"Berkun's guide to innovation is straightforward, succinct, and highly engaging. Use once and be glad. Use regularly and dramatically increase your odds of success."

—*Douglas K. Smith, coauthor of* Fumbling the Future: How Xerox Invented, Then Ignored, the First Personal Computer

"Berkun's book is a readable analysis of the history of innovation and popular misconceptions. His myth debunking will help innovators, managers of innovative teams, or funders of innovative activities. I'm buying copies for my entire lab."

—*Michael N. Nitabach, Assistant Professor, Department of Cellular Physiology, Yale University School of Medicine*

The
Myths of
Innovation

The
Myths of
Innovation

Scott Berkun

O'REILLY®

Beijing · Cambridge · Farnham · Köln · Sebastopol · Taipei · Tokyo

The Myths of Innovation
by Scott Berkun

Published by O'Reilly Media, Inc., 1005 Gravenstein Highway North, Sebastopol, CA 95472.

O'Reilly books may be purchased for educational, business, or sales promotional use. Online editions are also available for most titles (*http://my.safaribooksonline.com*). For more information, contact our corporate/institutional sales department: (800) 998-9938 or *corporate@oreilly.com*.

Editor: Mary Treseler
Production Editor:
   Rachel Monaghan
Copyeditor: Marlowe Shaeffer
Proofreader: Sada Preisch

Indexer: Ellen Troutman Zaig
Cover Designer: Mark Paglietti
Interior Designer: Ron Bilodeau
Illustrator: Robert Romano

Printing History:

August 2010:   First Edition.

This paperback edition is updated and expanded from the 2007 hardcover version, also published by O'Reilly.

ISBN: 978-1-449-38962-8

[F]

Contents

Commitment to research accuracy xiii

Preface for the paperback edition xv

Chapter 1
The myth of epiphany 1

Chapter 2
We understand the history of innovation .. 17

Chapter 3
There is a method for innovation 35

Chapter 4
People love new ideas 53

Chapter 5
The lone inventor 69

Chapter 6
Good ideas are hard to find 83

Chapter 7
Your boss knows more about
innovation than you 97

Chapter 8
The best ideas win **111**

Chapter 9
Problems and solutions **127**

Chapter 10
Innovation is always good **139**

Chapter 11
Epilogue: Beyond hype and history **153**

Chapter 12
Creative thinking hacks **167**

Chapter 13
How to pitch an idea **175**

Chapter 14
How to stay motivated **187**

Appendix
Research and recommendations **193**

Photo credits **205**

Acknowledgments **207**

How to help this book: A request from the author .. **211**

About the author **213**

Index **215**

Commitment to research accuracy

In the original edition of this book, I took great pains to get the facts, sources, and references right. However, as you'll learn in Chapter 2, history is more challenging than we think it is.

In this paperback edition, we corrected more than 40 issues, from typos to misreferences to clarifications of facts from history. They were mostly minor issues that were easy to correct. In some cases, I found better evidence and more accessible references.

But one can never be sure. It is possible, despite enlisting the help of an army of fact-checkers, that I have misrepresented facts or distorted the work of others, or that new evidence will surface that contradicts the facts I use. I promise that any oversights are unintentional. More importantly, I believe my arguments and the thoughts they provoke are valuable despite any inaccuracies.

As I've committed to in the past, I'll do my best to collect and review any corrections or improved references as I'm made aware of them.

All of the URLs and references found in this book will be available online for easier access. Visit *www.mythsofinnovation.com* to either report issues or make use of the references for further study. If you find an issue that has not been listed, please report it at the above URL for other readers' benefit and my own.

Preface for the paperback edition

*By idolizing those whom we honor,
we do a disservice both to them and
to ourselves...we fail to recognize
that we could go and do likewise.*
—Charles V. Willie

The other day, while dropping off my dry cleaning at the laundromat, I noticed a bright neon sign. It read, "Innovative dry-cleaning service," which, given my authorship of this book, piqued my curiosity. With shirts and pants in hand, I went to the counter and inquired, "So tell me, what are your dry-cleaning innovations?" The young lady behind the register offered only a blank stare. I had to point to the sign and explain what the word meant before she acknowledged, as if I were an idiot, that it was just marketing. As far as she knew, as daughter of the store's owner, there was nothing innovative in how they cleaned clothes (nor how they helped customers).

The word *innovation* has fallen on hard times. There is no innovation superhero, flying around at innovative speeds, using innovative ninja moves to prevent abuse of the word. Simply saying something is great doesn't make it so, yet as the success of marketing and advertising demonstrates, this doesn't stop people from trying. The i-word is thrown around so frequently it no longer means anything.

Today, and for a long time, the majority of what most people believe about ideas—from where they originate to how they are made into things that change the world—is based on sketchy sources. We watch movies featuring the success stories, and we hear legendary tales of geniuses and their flashes of insight, tales passed down from generation to generation, but few go back to see whether any of those stories actually happened. And when we try to work with ideas ourselves, we experience a reality so distant from what we've been taught to expect that it's easy to give up. Even if we fight through the confusion, we're chasing our guesses about what the process is supposed to be like. My goal is to turn all of this around.

I've spent years studying the history of creative thinking, especially around invention and entrepreneurship, digging up the truths behind the legends. I wanted to uncover what really happened because I believed knowing the truth would give me the greatest chances of learning and improving my own abilities, and teaching others to do the same. Each chapter explores one of the 10 most pervasive and misleading myths, reveals the facts, and offers advice and wisdom that you can apply to your own work.

This is the book, based on evidence rather than wishful thinking, I wish someone had given me when I started my career almost 20 years ago.

Before I get out of your way so you can begin Chapter 1, I need to say one last thing about the word *innovation*. It's not a word I'm fond of. It's used all too often today, and it has lost any significance. More useful to you, perhaps, is that of its many meanings you'll find in a dictionary, the most potent is *significant positive change*. If the thing offered represents a significant positive change for whomever it is offered to, by definition, it's an innovation. This calls into question statements such as "We innovate every day" or "We are in the innovation business," because if something is done regularly, how can it represent significant change? Even if it's possible, the turmoil that rate of change would create is unlikely to be positive (except for the handful of people who profit from the chaos). I carry a chip on my shoulder for anyone who uses the word innovation too often.

This definition also burdens creators to understand the recipients' perspective of whatever they make. If it's a positive change for the customer, even if the ideas being used have been around for years, it's an innovation to them. This is great: before anyone can call something an innovation, they need to find happy customers who would also use that label for it (or who would say, "This is a significant positive change!"). This might just mean that what's old and tired to you is the new hotness to someone else. Over a billion people in the world don't have electricity or clean drinking water. If you put a working 7-Eleven mini-mart, with refrigeration, plumbing, and WiFi Internet access next to their hut, they'd certainly call the store, and everything inside, an innovation. And by the same token, if a space alien landed in your backyard with an old, broken-down warp engine, something he and all his alien buddies have had for years, it would still be an innovation to you.

To practice what I preach, the word innovation appeared in the hardcover edition of this book about 65 times, down from 150 in the early manuscript. For this paperback edition, I added four new chapters focused on putting ideas to work, which raised that count slightly.[1] Tracking the word was a specific goal because it

---

[1] Three of the four chapters are heavily revised essays that originally appeared on *www.scottberkun.com*.

forced me to communicate clearly. I recommend you and your colleagues do the same; for example, if you mean "We want our business to grow," say it—don't mask the meaning by using the i-word. If you want to be perceived as being a creative company, fine. Perhaps your ambition is to make products that lead in market share, or to have passionate, happy customers. Excellent. Write those exact words down. Reserve the i-word for...nothing. In the few instances where you are honestly taking the big risks necessary to achieve significant positive change, talk about what those risks are and what the positive changes will be. The specifics of what you mean will inspire and empower more people than any overused business-school marketing jargon ever could.

Be well, be bold, and have fun—I hope to see you next time I'm on tour.

—Scott Berkun
Seattle, Washington, USA
August 2010

CHAPTER 1

The myth of epiphany

While waiting in the lobby of Google's main building, I snuck into the back of a tour group heading inside. These outsiders, a mix of executives and business managers, had the giddy looks of kids in a candy factory—their twinkling eyes captivated by Google's efforts to make a creative workplace. My clandestine activities unnoticed, we strolled together under the high ceilings and brightly colored open spaces designed to encourage inventiveness. No room or walkway was free of beanbag chairs, ping-pong tables, laptops, and Nerf toys, and we saw an endless clutter of shared games, brain-teasing puzzles, and customized tech gadgetry. The vibe was a happy blend of the MIT Media Lab, the Fortune 500, and an eccentrically architected private library, with young, smart, smiley people lingering just about everywhere. To those innocents on the tour, perhaps scarred survivors of cubicle careers, the sights at Google were mystical—a working wonderland. And their newfound Google awe was the perfect cover for me to tag along, observing their responses to this particular approach to the world of ideas (see Figure 1-1).

Figure 1-1. One of the creative interiors of Google's main campus in Mountain View, California.

The tour, which I took in 2006 after they moved to their Mountain View headquarters, offered fun facts about life at Google, like the free organic lunches in the cafeteria and power outlets for lap-tops in curious places (stairwells, for example), expenses taken to ensure Googlers are able, at all times, to find their best ideas. While I wondered whether Beethoven or Hemingway, great minds noted for thriving on conflict, could survive in such a nurturing environment without going postal, my attention was drawn to questions from the tourists. A young professional woman, barely containing her embarrassment, asked, "Where is the search engine? Are we going to see it?", at which only half the group laughed. (There is no singular "engine"—only endless dull bays of server computers running the search-engine software.)

The second question, though spoken in private, struck home. A 30-something man turned to his tour buddy, leaning in close to whisper. I strained to overhear without looking like I was eaves-dropping. He pointed to the young programmers in the distance, and behind a cupped hand, he questioned, "I see them talking and typing, but when do they come up with their ideas?" His buddy stood tall and looked around, as if to discover something his friend had missed: a secret passageway, epiphany machines, or perhaps a circle of black-robed geniuses casting creativity spells. Finding nothing, he shrugged. They sighed, the tour moved on, and I escaped to consider my observations.

The question of where ideas come from is on the mind of anyone visiting a research lab, an artist's workshop, or an inventor's studio. It's the secret we hope to see—the magic that happens when new things are born. Even in environments geared for cre-ativity like Google, staffed with the best and brightest, the elusive nature of ideas leaves us restless. We want creativity to be like opening a soda can or taking a bite of a sandwich: mechanical things that are easy to observe. Yet, simultaneously, we hold ideas to be special and imagine that their creation demands something beyond what we see every day. The result is that tours of amazing places, even with full access to creators themselves, never convince us that we've seen the real thing. We still believe in our hearts there are top-secret rooms behind motion-sensor security systems or bank-vault doors where ideas are neatly stacked up like bars of gold.

For centuries before Google, MIT, and IDEO—modern hotbeds of innovation—we struggled to explain any kind of creation, from the universe itself to the multitudes of ideas around us. While we can make atomic bombs and dry-clean silk ties, we still don't have satisfying answers for simple questions like: Where do songs come from? Is there an infinite variety of possible kinds of cheese? How did Shakespeare and Stephen King create so much, while we're satisfied watching sitcom reruns? Our popular answers have been unconvincing, enabling misleading, fantasy-laden myths to flourish.

One grand myth is the story of Isaac Newton and the discovery of gravity. As it's often told, Newton was sitting under a tree, an apple fell on his head, and the idea of gravity was born. It's entertaining more than truthful, turning the mystery of ideas into something innocent, obvious, and comfortable. Instead of hard work, personal risk, and sacrifice, the myth suggests that great ideas come to people who are lucky enough to be in the right place at the right time. The catalyst of the story isn't even a person: it's the sad, nameless, suicidal apple.

It's disputed whether Newton ever observed an apple fall. He certainly was never struck by one, unless there's secret evidence of fraternity food fights while he was studying in Cambridge. Even if the apple incident took place, the legend discounts Newton's 20 years of work to explain gravity. Just as Columbus didn't discover America, Newton did not actually discover gravity—the Egyptian pyramids and Roman coliseums prove that people understood the concept well before Newton. Rather, he used math to explain more precisely than anyone before him how gravity works. While this contribution is certainly important, it's not the same as discovery.

The best possible truth to take from the apple myth is that Newton was a deeply curious man who spent time observing things in the world. He watched the stars in the sky and studied how light moved through air, all as part of his scientific work to understand the world. It was no accident that he studied gravity. Even if the myth were true and he did see an apple fall, he made so many other observations based on ordinary things that his thinking couldn't have been solely inspired by fruity accidents in the park.

Newton's apple myth is a story of epiphany or "a sudden manifestation of the essence or meaning of something,"[1] and in the mythology of innovation, epiphanies serve an important purpose.

---

1 This approximates the third entry in *Merriam-Webster's* online listing. The first two are religious in nature: *http://www.m-w.com/dictionary/epiphany.*

The word has religious origins, and it initially meant that all insight came by divine power. This isn't surprising because most early theologians,[2] including Christians, defined God as the sole creative force in the universe. As a rule, people believed that if it's creative, it's divine, but if it's derivative, it's human. Had you asked the first maker of the wheel[3] for an autograph, he'd likely be offended that you'd want his name instead of his god's (one wonders what he'd think of Mr. Goodyear and his eponymous tires).[4]

Today, we use epiphany without awareness of its heavy-duty heritage, as in "I had an epiphany for rearranging my closet." While the religious connotations are forgotten, the implications remain: we're hinting that we don't know where the idea came from and won't take credit for it. Even the language we use to describe ideas—that they *come* to us or that we have to *find* them—implies that they exist outside of us, beyond our control. This way of thinking is helpful when we want to assuage our guilt over blank sheets of paper where love letters, business plans, and novels are supposed to be, but it does little to improve our innate creative talents.

The Greeks were so committed to ideas as supernatural forces that they created an entire group of goddesses (not one but nine) to represent creative power; the opening lines of both *The Iliad* and *The Odyssey* begin with calls to them.[5] These nine goddesses, or *muses*, were the recipients of prayers from writers, engineers, and musicians. Even the great minds of the time, like Socrates and Plato, built shrines and visited temples dedicated to their particular muse (or muses, for those who hedged their bets). Right now, under our very secular noses, we honor these beliefs in our language, as the etymology of words like museum ("place of the muses") and music ("art of the muses") come from the Greek heritage of ideas as superhuman forces.

2　Robert S. Albert and Mark A. Runco, "A History of Research on Creativity," in *Handbook of Creativity*, ed. Robert J. Sternberg (Cambridge University Press, 1998), 16–20.

3　The wheel's prehistoric origins are a misnomer. The first wheels used for any practical purpose date back to around 3500 BCE. Start with *http://www.ideafinder. com/history/inventions/wheel.htm*.

4　The rubber tire was once a big innovation, and the history of Goodyear is a surprisingly good read: *http://www.goodyear.com/corporate/history/history_ overview.html*.

5　Homer, *The Iliad* (Penguin Classics Deluxe Edition, 1998), and *The Odyssey* (Penguin Classics Deluxe Edition, 1999).

When amazing innovations arise and change the world today, the first stories about them mirror the myths from the past. Putting accuracy aside in favor of echoing the epiphany myth, reporters and readers first move to tales of magic moments. Tim Berners-Lee, the man who invented the World Wide Web, explained:

> *Journalists have always asked me what the crucial idea was or what the singular event was that allowed the Web to exist one day when it hadn't before. They are frustrated when I tell them there was no Eureka moment. It was not like the legendary apple falling on Newton's head to demonstrate the concept of gravity...it was a process of accretion (growth by gradual addition).[6]*

No matter how many times he relayed the dedicated hours of debate over the Web's design, and the various proposals and iterations of its development, it's the myth of magic that journalists and readers desperately want to uncover.

When the founders of the eBay Corporation[7] began, they struggled for attention and publicity from the media. Their true story, that they desired to create a perfect market economy where individuals could freely trade with each other, was too academic to interest reporters. It was only when they invented a quasi-love story—about how the founder created the company so his fiancée could trade PEZ dispensers—that they got the press coverage they wanted. The truer story of market economies wasn't as palatable as a tale of muse-like inspiration between lovers. The PEZ story was one of the most popular company inception stories told during the late 1990s, and it continues to be told despite confessions from the founders. Myths are often more satisfying to us than the truth, which explains their longevity and resistance to facts: we *want* to believe that they're true. This begs the question: is shaping the truth into the form of an epiphany myth a kind of lie, or is it just smart PR?

Even the tale of Newton's apple owes its mythic status to the journalists of the day. Voltaire and other popular 18th-century writers spread the story in their essays and letters. An eager public, happy to hear the ancient notion of ideas as magic, endorsed and embellished the story (e.g., the apple's trajectory moved over time, from being

---

6 Tim Berners-Lee, *Weaving the Web* (HarperCollins, 1999).

7 Adam Cohen, *The Perfect Store: Inside eBay* (Back Bay Books, 2003).

observed in the distance to landing at his feet to eventually striking Newton's head in a telling by Isaac D'Israeli[8] decades later). While it is true that by dramatizing Newton's work Voltaire helped popularize Newton's ideas, two centuries later little of Newton's process is remembered: myths always serve promotion more than education. Anyone wishing to innovate must seek better sources and can easily start by examining the history of any idea.

Ideas never stand alone

The computer keyboard I'm typing on now involves dozens of ideas and inventions. It's composed of the typewriter, electricity, plastics, written language, operating systems, circuits, USB connectors, and binary data. If you eliminated any of these things from the history of the universe, the keyboard in front of me (as well as the book in front of you) would disappear. The keyboard, like all innovations, is a combination of things that existed before. The combination might be novel, or used in an original way, but the materials and ideas all existed in some form somewhere before the first keyboard was made. Similar games can be played with cell phones (telephones, computers, and radio waves), fluorescent lights (electric power, advanced glass moldings, and some basic chemistry), and GPS navigation (space flight, high-speed networks, atomic clocks). Any seemingly grand idea can be divided into an infinite series of smaller, previously known ideas. An entire television series called *Connections* (by science historian James Burke) was dedicated to exploring the theme of the surprising relationships between ideas and their interconnectedness throughout history.[9] Similar patterns exist in the work of innovation itself. For most, there is no singular magic moment; instead, there are many smaller insights accumulated over time. The Internet required nearly 40 years of innovations in electronics, networking, and packet-switching software before it even approximated the system Tim Berners-Lee used to create the World Wide Web.[10] The refrigerator, the laser, and the dishwasher were disasters for decades before enough of the cultural and technological barriers

---

[8] Isaac D'Israeli, *Curiosities of Literature: With a View of the Life and Writings of the Author* (Widdleton, 1872).

[9] *http://en.wikipedia.org/wiki/Connections_(TV_series)*.

[10] See the Internet Timeline: *http://www.pbs.org/opb/nerds2.0.1/timeline/*.

were eliminated through various insights, transforming the products into true business innovations. Big thoughts are fun to romanticize, but it's many small insights coming together that bring big ideas into the world.

However, it's often not until people try their own hands at innovation or entrepreneurship that they see past the romance and recognize the real challenges. It's easy to read shallow, mythologized accounts of what Leonardo da Vinci, Thomas Edison, or Jeff Bezos did, and make the mistake of mimicking their behavior in an entirely different set of circumstances (or with comparatively modest intellects). The myths are so strong that it's a surprise to many to learn that having one big idea isn't enough to succeed. Instead of wanting to innovate, a process demanding hard work and many ideas, most want to have innovated. The myth of epiphany tempts us to believe that the magic moment is the grand catalyst; however, all evidence points to its more supportive role.

One way to think about epiphany is to imagine working on a jigsaw puzzle. When you put the last piece into place, is there anything special about that last piece or what you were wearing when you put it in? The only reason that last piece is significant is because of the other pieces you'd already put into place. If you jumbled up the pieces a second time, any one of them could turn out to be the last, magical piece. Epiphany works the same way: it's not the apple or the magic moment that matters much, it's the work before and after (see Figure 1-2).

The magic feeling at the moment of insight, when the last piece falls into place, comes for two reasons. The first reason is that it's the reward for many hours (or years) of investment coming together. In comparison to the simple action of fitting the puzzle piece into place, we feel the larger collective payoff of hundreds of pieces' worth of work. The second reason is that innovative work isn't as predictable as jigsaw puzzles, so there's no way to know when the moment of insight will come. It's a surprise. Like hiking up a strange mountain through cold, heavy fog, you never know how much farther you have to go to reach the top. When suddenly the air clears and you're at the summit, it's overwhelming. You hoped it was coming, but you couldn't be certain when or if it would happen, and the emotional payoff is hard to match (explaining both why people climb mountains and invent new things).

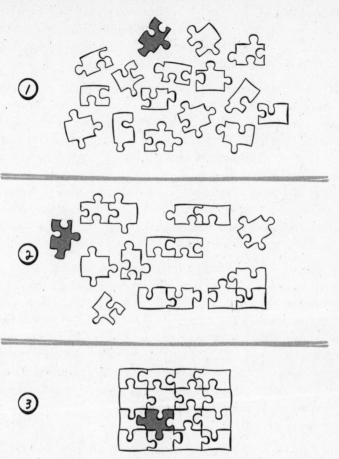

Figure 1-2. Epiphany is the moment when the last piece of work fits into place. However, the last piece isn't any more magical than the others, and it has no magic without its connection to the other pieces.

Gordon Gould, the primary inventor of the laser, had this to say about his own epiphany:

> In the middle of one Saturday night...the whole thing...suddenly popped into my head and I saw how to build the laser...but that flash of insight required the 20 years of work I had done in physics and optics to put all of the bricks of that invention in there.

Any major innovation or insight can be seen in this way. It's simply the final piece of a complex puzzle falling into place. But unlike a puzzle, the universe of ideas can be combined in an infinite number of ways, so part of the challenge of innovation is coming up with the problem to solve, not just its solution. The pieces used to innovate one day can be reused and reapplied to innovate again, only to solve a different problem.

The other great legend of innovation and epiphany is the tale of Archimedes' Eureka. As the story goes, the great inventor Archimedes was asked by his king to detect whether a gift was made of false gold. One day, Archimedes took a bath, and on observing the displacement of water as he stepped in, he recognized a new way to look at the problem: by knowing an object's volume and weight, he could compute its density. He ran naked into the streets yelling "Eureka!"—*I have found it*—and perhaps scandalizing confused onlookers into curious thoughts about what exactly he had been looking for.

The part of the story that's overlooked, like Newton's apple tale, is that Archimedes spent significant time trying and failing to find solutions to the problem before he took the bath. The history is sketchy at best, but I suspect he took the bath as stress relief from the various pressures of innovation.[11] Unlike Google employees, or the staff at the MIT Media Lab, he didn't have friends with Nerf weapons or sand volleyball courts where he could blow off steam. So, as is common in myths of epiphany, we are told where he was when the last piece fell into place, but nothing about how the other pieces got there.

In Mihaly Csikszentmihalyi's book, *Creativity: Flow and the Psychology of Discovery and Invention*,[12] he studied the thought processes of nearly 100 creative people, from artists to scientists, including notables like Robertson Davies, Stephen Jay Gould, Don Norman, Linus Pauling, Jonas Salk, Ravi Shankar, and Edward O. Wilson. Instead of doing clinical research with probes and brain scans, he focused instead on the innovators' individual insights. He wanted to understand their perceptions of innovation, unfiltered by the often stifling and occasionally self-defeating rigors of hard science.

---

11 The most well-known version of the Eureka story comes in the form of a legend in Vitruvius' *Ten Books of Architecture* (Dover, 1960), 253–255. This book is the first pattern language of design in Western history, documenting the Roman architecture techniques of Vitruvius' time.

12 Mihaly Csikszentmihalyi, *Creativity: Flow and the Psychology of Discovery and Invention* (HarperPerennial, 1997).

One goal was to understand epiphany and how it happens; through his research, he observed a common pattern. Epiphany had three parts, roughly described as early, insight, and after.[13] During the early period, hours or days are spent understanding the problem and immersing oneself in the domain. An innovator might ask questions like "What else in the world is like this?" and "Who has solved a problem similar to mine?", learning everything he can and exploring the world of related ideas. And then there is a period of incubation in which the knowledge is digested, leading to experiments and rough attempts at solutions. Sometimes there are long pauses during incubation when progress stalls and confidence wanes, an experience the Greeks would have called "losing the muse."

The big insights, if they happen, occur in the depths of incubation; it's possible these pauses are minds catching up with everything they've observed. Csikszentmihalyi explains that deep quiet periods, time spent doing unrelated things, often helps new ideas surface. He writes, "Cognitive accounts of what happens during incubation assume...that some kind of information processing keeps going on even when we are not aware of it, even while we are asleep." Our subconscious minds play large roles in creative thinking: they may be the sources for the unexplained insights we romanticize. When a promising idea surfaces out of the subconscious and rises into our active minds, it can feel like it came from somewhere else because we weren't aware of our subconscious thoughts while we were mowing the lawn.

The best lesson from the myths of Newton and Archimedes is to work passionately but to take breaks. Sitting under trees and relaxing in baths lets the mind wander and frees the subconscious to do work on our behalf.[14] Freeman Dyson, a world-class physicist and author, agrees: "I think it's very important to be idle...people who keep themselves busy all the time are generally not creative. So I am not ashamed of being idle." This isn't to justify surfing instead of studying: it's only when activities are done

---

[13] Csikszentmihalyi describes epiphany in five phases, but I've simplified it to three for the purposes of this chapter.

[14] There is neuroscience research that supports the importance of daydreaming in creativity; see *http://www.boston.com/bostonglobe/ideas/articles/2008/08/31/daydream_achiever/*.

as breaks that the change of activity pays off. Some workaholic innovators tweak this by working on multiple projects at the same time, effectively using work on one project as a break from the other. Edison, Darwin, da Vinci, Michelangelo, and van Gogh all regularly switched between different projects, occasionally in different fields, possibly accelerating an exchange of ideas and seeding their minds for new insights.

One of the truths of both Newton's apple tale and Archimedes' bathtub story is that triggers for breakthroughs can come from ordinary places. There is research indicating that creative people more easily make connections between unrelated ideas.[15] Richard Feynman curiously observed students spinning plates in the Cornell University cafeteria and eventually related the mathematics of this behavior to an unsolved problem in quantum physics, earning him the Nobel Prize. Picasso found a trashed bicycle and rearranged its seat and handlebars, converting it into a masterpiece sculpture of a bull. The idea of observation as the key to insight, rather than IQ scores or intellectual prowess, is best captured by something da Vinci—whose famous technological inventions were inspired by observing nature—wrote hundreds of years ago:

> Stand still and watch the patterns, which by pure chance have been generated: Stains on the wall, or the ashes in a fireplace, or the clouds in the sky, or the gravel on the beach or other things. If you look at them carefully you might discover miraculous inventions.

In psychology books, the talent for taking two unrelated concepts and finding connections between them is called associative ability. In his book *Creativity in Science: Change, Logic, Genius, and Zeitgeist*, Dean Simonton points out that "persons with low associative barriers may think to connect ideas or concepts that have very little basis in past experience or that cannot easily be traced logically."[16] Read that last sentence again: it's indistinguishable from various definitions of insanity. The tightrope between being strange and being creative is too narrow to walk without occasionally landing on either side, explaining why so many great

---

15 Ibid.

16 Dean Keith Simonton, *Creativity in Science: Chance, Logic, Genius, and Zeitgeist* (Cambridge University Press, 2004).

minds are lampooned as eccentrics. Their willingness to try seemingly illogical ideas or to make connections others struggle to see invariably leads to judgment (and perhaps giving some truth to stereotypes of mad scientists and unpredictable artists). Developing new ideas requires questions and approaches that most people won't understand initially, which leaves many true innovators at risk of becoming lonely, misunderstood characters.

Beyond epiphany

If we had a list of the most amazing breakthrough insights that would change the world in the next decade, hard work would follow them all. No grand innovation in history has escaped the long hours required to take an insight and work it into a form useful to the world. It's one thing to imagine world peace or the Internet, something Vannevar Bush did in 1945 in a paper titled "As We May Think,"[17] but it's another to break down the idea into parts that can be built, or even attempted.

Csikszentmihalyi describes this part of innovation, the elaboration of an idea into function, as "the one that takes up the most time and involves the hardest work." Scientists need to not only make discoveries, but to provide enough research to prove to others that the discoveries are valid. Newton was far from the first to consider a system of gravity, but he was the only one to complete the years of work to produce an accurate one in his day. *Star Trek*, a television program in the '60s, had the idea for cell phones, but it took decades for technology to be developed and refined to the point where such a thing could be practical (and, of course, many of *Star Trek's* sci-fi ideas have yet to be realized). Not to mention the services and businesses that are needed to make the devices affordable to consumers around the world. The big ideas are a small part of the process of true innovation.

The most useful way to think of epiphany is as an occasional bonus of working on tough problems. Most innovations come without epiphanies, and when a powerful moment does happen, little knowledge is granted for how to find the next one. Even in

---

[17] Bush's paper is a recommended read. It goes beyond hyperbole and breaks down a vision into smaller, practical problems (a hint for today's visionaries): *http:// www.theatlantic.com/doc/194507/bush.*

the myths, Newton had one apple and Archimedes had one Eureka. To focus on the magic moments is to miss the point. The goal isn't the magic moment: it's the end result of a useful innovation. Ted Hoff, the inventor of the first microprocessor (Intel's 4004), explained, "If you're always waiting for that wonderful breakthrough, it's probably never going to happen. Instead, what you have to do is keep working on things. If you find something that looks good, follow through with it."[18]

Nearly every major innovation of the 20th century took place without claims of epiphany. The World Wide Web, the web browser, the computer mouse, and the search engine—four pivotal developments in the history of business and technology—all involved long sequences of innovation, experimentation, and discovery. They demanded contributions from dozens of different individuals and organizations, and took years (if not decades) to reach fruition. The makers of Mosaic and Netscape, the first popular web browsers, didn't invent them from nothing. There had been various forms of hypertext browsers for decades, and they applied some of those ideas to the new context of the Internet. The founders of Google did not invent the search engine—they were years late for that honor. As the founders of Amazon.com, the most well-known survivor of the late-'90s Internet boom, explain, "There wasn't this sense of 'My God. We've invented this incredible thing that nobody else has seen before, and it'll just take over.'"[19] Instead they, like most innovators, recognized a set of opportunities—scientific, technological, or entrepreneurial—and set about capitalizing on them.

Peter Drucker, in *Innovation and Entrepreneurship*,[20] offers advice for anyone in any pursuit awaiting the muse:

> *Successful entrepreneurs do not wait until "the Muse kisses them" and gives them a "bright idea": they go to work. Altogether they do not look for the "biggie," the innovation that will "revolutionize the industry," create a "billion-dollar business" or "make one rich over-night." Those entrepreneurs who start*

---

18 Kenneth A. Brown, *Inventors at Work: Interviews with 16 Notable American Inventors* (Microsoft Press, 1988).

19 Paul Barton-Davis, quoted in Robert Spector, *Amazon.com: Get Big Fast* (HarperBusiness, 2000), 48.

20 Peter Drucker, *Innovation and Entrepreneurship* (Collins, 1993).

*out with the idea that they'll make it big—and in a hurry—can
be guaranteed failure. They are almost bound to do the wrong
things. An innovation that looks very big may turn out to be
nothing but technical virtuosity; and innovation with modest
intellectual pretensions, a McDonald's, for instance, may turn
into gigantic, highly profitable businesses.*

The same can be said for any successful scientist, technologist, or
innovator. What matters is the ability to see a problem clearly,
combined with the talent to solve it. Both of those tasks are generally defined, however unglamorously, as work. Epiphany, for all
its graces, is largely irrelevant because it can't be controlled. Even
if there existed an epiphany genie, granting big ideas to worthy
innovators, the innovators would still have piles of rather ordinary work to do to actualize those ideas. It is an achievement to
find a great idea, but it is an even greater achievement to successfully use it to improve the world.

CHAPTER 2

We understand the history of innovation

*History is written by those who win and
those who dominate.*

—Edward Said

History is the lie commonly agreed upon.

—Voltaire

*History is a damn dim candle
over a damn dark abyss.*

—W. S. Holt

*History is indeed the witness of the times,
the light of truth.*

—Cicero

In the Egyptian wing of London's British Museum, I hovered by
the Rosetta Stone, waiting for the guards to look away. When a
child stumbled over the corner of a lesser relic, distracting the
guards, I moved in. Holding my breath, I reached over the steel
barrier, stretched out my trembling hand, and ran it across the letters on the Stone.[1] My fingertips gently stroked the cold surface,
racing along ancient corners of mysterious symbols: in one
motion, I touched more history than fills many men's dreams.
With my hand back at my side, I strolled away, ashamed and
thrilled, praying against alarms and handcuffs that never came. I
didn't wash that hand all day, lost in imagining the important men
behind the Stone (see Figure 2-1).

But when the thrill of my museum mischief faded, one frustration
remained: the Stone is famous for reasons irrelevant to those who
conceived it. The stonecutters could not have imagined their work
in a European museum 2,000 years in the future, with hired
guards protecting it from hooligans like me. Yet, there it sat, as if
its destiny was to be found in a rubble pile by the French, used to
decipher hieroglyphics, and, finally, displayed in its true resting
place in London. In the solemn, shrine-like atmosphere of the
museum, I'd forgotten that the Stone is an artifact: it's an object
that was part of history but not history itself.

---

[1] Today, the Stone is encased in glass. It was cleaned in 1998, removing layers of
wax, inks, and oils collected over years of imprints, copies, and immature (cough)
human patrons. The Stone is made of a substance similar to granite, immune to
the negative effects of curious paws. On principle, I've since resisted the urge to
make unauthorized contact with all relics, including history professors.

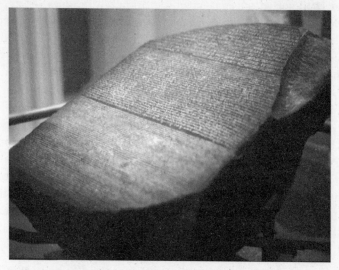

Figure 2-1. The Rosetta Stone at the British Museum, circa 1996.

Although the Stone is more of a discovery than an invention, this gap between how the stonemakers saw their work and how we see it today is meaningful to innovators. To understand innovations as they happen, we need to see how history changes perceptions and re-examine events like the discovery of the Rosetta Stone.

Weighing nearly 2,000 pounds, the Stone is a fragment of an Egyptian pillar created in 196 BCE. In its time, the Stone was ordinary, one of many used by pharaohs to communicate with their people. The message on the Stone—the rarely mentioned reason it was made—is a public service announcement, mostly praising the pharaoh ("the new king, great in glory, the stabilizer of Egypt, pious in matters of gods, superior to his adversaries..."). The Stone is of minor interest save two facts:

1. When the Stone was found in 1789, we were clueless about hieroglyphics.

2. It was the first object found with writing in both hieroglyphics and Greek, making translation possible.

It's a wondrous thing given our situation, but these facts have nothing to do with the making of the Stone—they're circumstances that developed lifetimes after its creation.

If we had sorted out hieroglyphics through other means, say, by discovering an Egyptian-to-Greek translation book in Athens (possible, as the Greeks ruled Egypt for decades),[2] or finding another document written in multiple languages, it would have served the same purpose, and would now be sitting in the museum instead of the Stone (e.g., "The Rosetta recipe for Egyptian meatloaf"). So while the Stone deserves a first-rate exhibit in the British Museum, its value derives from great circumstances. The best lesson it offers is that ordinary things, people, and events are transformed into legends by the forces of time. Who knows: if I bury my beat-up third-rate cell phone in the right ditch in Paris, a million years from now, it might be the grand museum exhibit on some alien planet, as the cornerstone to (mis)understanding the human race ("Here, behind space-glass, is the historic Parisian Phone").

What does all this have to do with innovation? Well, take one great innovation: the printing press. More than 500 years after his death, Johannes Gutenberg is heralded as one of the most important people in history. He's ranked above Einstein, Aristotle, and Moses in one list of the most influential people of all time.[3] Despite the fact that the Chinese invented movable type and many print techniques centuries earlier, Gutenberg was the first to succeed with them in Europe.[4] Today, we can trace the existence of websites and bestsellers directly to the work in his shop in Mainz, Germany.

However, the deception (by omission) in Gutenberg's story is that his influence was not felt in his lifetime. He wasn't a hero of his age, and, like the makers of the Rosetta Stone, his intentions were not the same as those for which we credit him today. He was not trying to free the world through access to knowledge or to pave the way for the Internet Age—as best as we can tell, he was simply trying and failing to make a living.[5] Like the stonecutters, Gutenberg was a

---

2 The famed library of Alexandria, the largest library of ancient times, may have had various tomes on translating hieroglyphics, but it was destroyed (probably in the 4th century): *http://www.bbc.co.uk/history/ancient/egyptians/*.

3 Based on the 1992 book by Michael H. Hart, *The 100*: *http://www.answers.com/topic/the-100*. *Time*'s 2006 Top 100 people lists a few innovation notables, including Jimmy Wales (Wikipedia), and Niklas Zennström and Janus Friis (Skype).

4 John Man, *Gutenberg: How One Man Remade the World with Words* (Wiley, 2002).

5 Ibid. We do know about his life from court and business records, which show many failed projects and one major lawsuit in which Gutenberg lost much of his work.

craftsman doing his job, and he couldn't have imagined that centuries after his death, millions of books and websites would be published annually, nor that they'd often mention his name.

His influence, similar to the impact of the Rosetta Stone, owes as much to circumstance, world politics, and chance as to his abilities as a printmaker. (The Chinese and Islamic civilizations both had the technological ingredients needed to achieve what Gutenberg did well before he was born, but it never came to be.[6]) Unlike with Michelangelo, da Vinci, or other notables of his time, few records of Gutenberg's life were kept, as his work and life weren't deemed important: it's by a string of fortunate events that we even know his name.[7]

In his time, his innovations were perceived in a radically different way than we see them now. This is a fact we in the present must understand: when the legends we know so well today, from Vincent van Gogh to Steve Jobs to Albert Einstein, were becoming legendary, they were rarely seen as legends.

However, the stories told in schools and books present Gutenberg and other innovators as obvious, logical, and necessary contributors to the world, begging the assumption that if we were alive in their time, we'd see them in the same way they're portrayed in our history books. Those glorified accounts present innovation in a distorted way that is impossible to achieve in the present because the neat arcs of progress, clear sense of purpose, and certainty of success are heavily shaped, if not invented, by hindsight.

Why does history seem perfect?

If you take a walk in 21st-century Rome, it's obvious that Romans were masterful builders. There are coliseums (see Figure 2-2), temples, baths, and aqueducts thousands of years old that are still standing (and in many cases still working). The problem is that we're biased by what we can't see. These buildings are the

---

6   The forces that made the difference were cultural and coincidental. Gutenberg made key advancements, but more significantly, the Chinese language had hundreds of characters, not 26, making printing systems harder to perfect. Gutenberg's work coincided with Luther's reformation of the Church, fueling interest in printing bibles—an interest that didn't surface in the East.

7   John Man, *Gutenberg: How One Man Remade the World with Words* (Wiley, 2002).

minority of what the Romans made: the others fell down or were built over and buried, or in some cases torn apart for materials used in other buildings, and are thus lost to history. While the Romans deserve praise for their engineering prowess, they were not perfect engineers—they made mistakes all the time. Their ruling class did live in the glorious marble structures depicted in movies, but most Romans lived in collapse-prone tenements that killed thousands.[8]

Figure 2-2. The ever-sturdy Roman Coliseum, built over the burned remains of Emperor Nero's Golden House.

Despite the wonderful domes and legendary straight roads, the great fire of Rome in 64 CE burned down two-thirds of the city, including the 800-year-old Temple of Jupiter and the Atrium Vestae, the most sacred shrine in the Roman Forum.[9] This means that most of the Rome we know today, ruins included, was built to replace the city that burned to the ground.

The lesson I'm hinting at is larger than Rome: examine any legend of innovation, from inventors to scientists to engineers, and you'll find that history has made similar natural omissions. History can't

---

8   Jerome Carcopino, *Daily Life in Ancient Rome—The People and the City at the Height of the Empire* (Yale University Press, 2003).

9   *http://www.pbs.org/wnet/secrets/case_rome/index.html.*

give attention to what's been lost, hidden, or deliberately buried; it is mostly a telling of success, not the partial failures that enabled success.[10] Without at least imagining the missing dimensions to the stories, our view of how to make things happen in the present is seriously compromised.

Recent history has similar problems. Most Americans are taught that Columbus was a hero who navigated dangerous seas to discover the place we call home, who fought for the supposedly innovative belief that the world was round. (This is a bizarre myth because sailors since ancient times knew the world was a sphere—they just didn't know how large it was.[11]) But reading Howard Zinn's *A People's History of the United States*[12] or James W. Loewen's *Lies My Teacher Told Me*[13] reveals other equally relevant, but less flattering, truths about Columbus, citing his grand incompetence, rampant greed, and involvement in genocide. Which view, hero or fool, is right? It seems they both are, but telling the truth requires more than the superficial paragraph historic figures like Columbus typically earn in textbooks. Perhaps worse, much like the myth of epiphany, we're fond of reading and writing histories that make us feel better about the present. Once learned, faith in those versions of history is hard to shake, no matter how convincing the alternatives.

Consider this: would you buy a book titled *Why the Past Is Frustrating, Embarrassing, and Uncertain: A Litany of 78 Labyrinthine Enigmas?* It's hard to imagine this title on a bestseller list or surviving a PTA review committee of material for elementary school students ("It will damage their little brains!", I can hear them crying). For all our interest in truth, we look to historians to

---

[10] In the case of Rome, few wrote about life in the tenements or chronicled engineering failures that occurred at the hands of the Roman elite (would you have published much about Caesar's or Nero's shortcomings?). Dissenting voices are rare in recorded history because few had the means to write (Rome was founded at least 1,500 years before Gutenberg's press). If history seems perfect, it's not because life made more sense to people then—it's because much is hidden about what happened and why.

[11] Aristotle was one of the first to suggest the idea, but any idiot in a boat observing the curve of the earth should be able to figure that out. The horizon is approximately five miles away, farther if you're elevated off the ground: *http://www-istp. gsfc.nasa.gov/stargaze/Scolumb.htm*.

[12] Howard Zinn, *A People's History of the United States* (HarperCollins, 1980).

[13] James W. Loewen, *Lies My Teacher Told Me* (Touchstone, 1996).

sort things out, so as not to confuse or anger us. Holding up the Romans as superhuman, mistake-free engineers, or Columbus as a hero, simplifies the world in the same way as the myth of epiphany: it makes innovation special and separate from our daily experience. The Rosetta Stone, Gutenberg's press, and Roman architecture—all innovations or breakthroughs in their own way—arrived through many failures, chance events, and contrivances of human nature, but those details kill the easy romance we crave.

Don't get me wrong: we should feel wonder when near the Rosetta Stone, Roman ruins, or any stepping-stone of innovation, but not because they're magical, otherworldly things (except, perhaps, the Egyptian pyramids, whose construction we still do not fully understand).[14] Instead, we should be inspired because these artifacts connect our personal struggles, glories, fears, and passions with those of the people who made the things we're so quick to put on a pedestal—that's the true power of history.

Even with this goal, there are problems with the process of history that all historians, for all their integrity and altruistic intentions, can't escape: they have biases and desires like the rest of us. Beyond the need to make a living and write things people will buy, every writer, no matter how many degrees or textbooks in her name, has an opinion and a point of view (including yours truly). Writers can't study every fact or empathize with every perspective. These problems are so serious to innovation and general history that historians have a discipline to study them called *historiography*. Edward Carr, a prominent historian in this field, wrote in his classic *What Is History?*:

> It used to be said that facts speak for themselves. This is of course untrue. The facts speak only when the historian calls on them: it is he who decides to which facts to give the floor and in what order or context…a fact is like a sack—it won't stand up till you've put something in it.[15]

The shocking secret, which explains why teachers torture children with endless trivia, is that there is no objective history. But teaching

---

14 Jonathan Shaw, "Who Built the Pyramids?", *Harvard Magazine* (July–August 2003), *http://www.harvardmagazine.com/on-line/070391.html*.

15 Edward Hallett Carr, *What Is History?* (Vintage, 1967).

material that is palatable to everyone demands eliminating perspective, opinion, and humanity, leaving limp, soulless, humorless, embarrassment-free facts. Good histories are written by historians who carefully use diverse sources and take positions, but all histories are still based on interpretations and points of view. The good news is that even with accepted facts for events, there will always be new history books every year. The further we move away from an event, the more perspective we have about what happened. Just because we know all the facts about how the Internet was invented, or what started WWII, doesn't mean the history of those things ends. The more facts we compare and connections we make, the richer and more powerful history becomes.

The result is that our interests, as students of innovation, diverge with those of many historians and the general population. We want to understand the challenges of the past as if we were there, trying to innovate in that time with those constraints. We seek tactics to reuse or mistakes to learn from: we don't want convenience—we want truth. And to that end, there's no greater myth worth dispelling in the history of innovation than the idea that progress happens in a straight line.

Evolution and innovation

The Rosetta Stone sat buried in the sand, forgotten and unloved, for nearly 2,000 years. There were no markers or maps that led Napoleon's army to find it on that day in July 1799.[16] There was plenty of time for someone else to destroy it, deface it, chisel it into pretty sculptures, or hide it where it could never be found.[17] Of course, we're fortunate that events turned out as they did, but back then, when the past was the present, there was every possibility for things to turn out differently. The discovery of the Rosetta Stone was not inevitable.

Yet, when we look at any history timeline, we're encouraged to believe that other outcomes were impossible. Because the events on timelines happened, regardless of how bizarre or unlikely, we

---

[16] E. A. Wallis Budge, *The Rosetta Stone* (Dover, 1989). And see *http://www. napoleon-series.org/research/miscellaneous/c_rosetta.html*.

[17] One story related to Napoleon and Egypt is that his army was responsible for the destruction of the Sphinx's nose. This tale is definitely a myth: there are drawings of the damaged nose that date decades before Napoleon's visit to Egypt.

view them today as predetermined. It's not our fault, and it's not the fault of timeline makers (as that's a tough job). The simple fact is that these simplifications make history easier to explain. That said, it's also deceptive: at every point in every timeline that will ever be published, there was as much uncertainty and possibility for change as there is today.

Consider how technology is taught in ages: first there was stone, then bronze, then iron; or, in the computer world, it's the ages of mainframes, personal computers, and the Internet. We label periods of time around discoveries/inventions, projecting onto the past an orderly map to what was average everyday confusion. The earlier adopters of bronze swords, chasing the wooden-spear-wielding masses away from their treasures, didn't see themselves as being in the "Bronze Age" any more than the first Macintosh users saw themselves as being in the "pre–Internet Age," or than we see ourselves as being in the "age before telepathy was cheap and fun" (or whatever amazing thing happens next). Like in the present, people in the past believed they had divorced themselves from history and were living on the edge of the future in a crazy place called *now*.

This leads to the divisive question, the terrifying test of awareness of innovation history: were the innovations of the past inevitable? Are the Internet, the automobile, and the cell phone the necessary and unavoidable conclusion of human invention up until this time? Many think so. The idea even has the fancy name *techno-evolutionism*, but as cool as that sounds, it's still wishful thinking.[18]

Innovation and evolution demystified

This misconception of technological evolution mirrors a fallacy about the evolution of life, the universe, and everything. The unspoken myth many place inside the theory of evolution is that it defines modern civilization as the best possible result of history, since we're still around. Many think of evolution as a pyramid or ladder, with humans at the top, the crowning achievement of the planet, or even the universe (see Figure 2-3). But evolutionary science doesn't support this; like the pre-Copernican solar system,

---

[18] *http://www.aber.ac.uk/media/Documents/tecdet/tdet10.html.*

putting us at the center or on top of everything sure sounds nice, but it's absurd.

Figure 2-3. *Evolution means only that what's on top is fit for the current environment, not that it's "better."*

Natural selection doesn't mean that what's on top is special, it means only that the current environment is favorable toward that thing. Watch the music charts: Johnny Cash's album *Live at San Quentin* was a bestseller when released in 1968. But for decades after it didn't make the top 50 until *Walk the Line*, a successful movie about Cash's life, was released in 2005 and the environment changed. The album—the exact recording made nearly 40 years earlier—flew back up the charts: the criteria for the fittest changed. Certainly evolution is more complex than pop music (or at least I hope so), but the shifting nature of what is dominant is similar.

While humans might be dominant today (though the ever-resilient insect population most species depend on might question this[19]), if the planet's temperature dropped by half, its nations blew everyone up, or a few medium-size asteroids crashed into the Atlantic, the fittest creatures wouldn't be us. We'd be gone, best known by the surviving descendents of cockroaches as cute stuffed animals, in the

---

[19] Edward O. Wilson, *The Diversity of Life* (Belknap Press, 1992).

same fashion we've eulogized our food chain–dominant predecessors, the dinosaurs.

I wish I had better news, but instead of a cozy timeline granting easy confidence in inevitable progress, there are no guarantees. The wonders of Greece and Rome didn't prevent our clumsy civilization-wide slide into the Dark Ages. Technologies are invented, lost, found, ignored, and then found again all the time. (For example, the secrets of concrete used in the Coliseum, shown in Figure 2-2, were lost when Rome fell, not to be rediscovered until the 1800s.[20]) Carr goes on to say, "No sane person ever believed in a kind of progress which advanced in an unbroken straight line without reverses and deviations and breaks in continuity." The dilemma is that, at any moment, it's difficult to know whether we're witnessing progress or merely, in a hill-climbing distraction, a short-term gain with negative long-term consequences. There have been many biological dead ends: more than 90% of all species in the history of the earth have become extinct, and that's after living for millions of years.[21]

Innovation follows: the reason we use mobile phones or personal computers isn't because they're necessarily better in the long run than smoke signals or cave paintings, or that they're at the top of an unshakable technology pyramid.[22] We've adopted them gradually and intuitively as part of the experiment that is life. Simply because one thing has replaced another doesn't mean that it improves on it in every respect, and as conditions change, the notion of *improved* does as well. This hypothesis is easy to test: study the history of any innovation—from catapults to telegraphs to laser beams and nanotechnology—and you'll find its invention and adoption is based on ordinary, selfish, and mostly short-term motivations. Mistakes and complexities are everywhere, and while some of what goes on could be called progress, rendering a straight line of progress through history is a kind of invention itself.

---

[20] Dick Teresi, *Lost Discoveries: The Ancient Roots of Modern Science—from the Babylonians to the Maya* (Simon & Schuster, 2002).

[21] "A history of extinction," World Resources Institute, *http://archive.wri.org/page. cfm?id=519*.

[22] A simple review of misconceptions about evolution: *http://evolution.berkeley.edu/ evosite/misconceps/IBladder.shtml*.

Consider the gas-powered automobile, one of the most dominant technologies ever. In *The Evolution of Technology*, George Basalla explains:

> There were no automotive experts at the turn of the century, only inventors and entrepreneurs following their hunches and enthusiasms and trying to convince potential car owners to buy their product. Given this situation, once the gasoline engine gained ascendancy, steamers and electrics were either forgotten or viewed as missteps along the road to automotive progress.[23]

Gasoline engines and automobiles were successful not because they'd lead us on the best path, or even because they were the best solutions for the problems of the day. They succeeded, in natural-selection fashion, due to the combined circumstances of that time. Traffic jams, pollution, road rage, and dependence on limited oil supplies all call into question the suitability of the innovation we still base our lives on.

Dominant designs dominate history

Pick your favorite hot technology of the moment. How many different competing products are there? When an innovation is in progress, there are always competitors. Entrepreneurs are drawn to new markets because they have at least as good a chance as anyone else, even if they have less funding or experience. But what we forget is that every innovation, from a jet aircraft to a paper clip, was once an open, competitive, experiment-rich playing field.

In *Mastering the Dynamics of Innovation*, James Utterback writes:

> It would be tempting to think that there is some predetermination to the emergence of dominant design—that automobiles with internal combustion engines were somehow exactly what the gods of transportation always meant for us to have, and that earlier experiments with electric and steam powered cars were misguided aberrations destined to go nowhere. The emergence of a dominant design is not necessarily predetermined, but is the result of the interplay between technical and market choices at any particular time.[24]

---

[23] George Basalla, *The Evolution of Technology* (Cambridge University Press, 2002).

[24] James M. Utterback, *Mastering the Dynamics of Innovation* (Harvard Business School Press, 1996).

And don't forget the negative influence of the six-pack of human shortcomings: greed, irrationality, short-sightedness, egotism, lack of imagination, and just plain stupidity. It's quaint to think cars have seatbelts or antilock brakes because of the monk-like rationality, forethought, and good spiritedness of our innovation predecessors, but it just isn't so.[25]

This means that every technology, from pacemakers to contact lenses, fluorescent lights to birth control pills, arrived through the same chaos seen in the hot technologies of today. Just because dominant designs developed before we were born, or in fields so far from our own that we're ignorant of their struggles, doesn't mean their arrival was predictable, orderly, or even in our best interest. Yet, the dominant designs, the victors of any innovative pursuit, are the ones that get most of history's positive attention (see Figure 2-4).

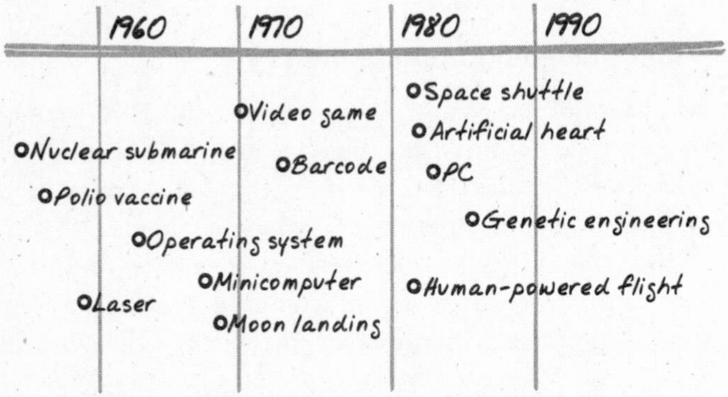

Figure 2-4. A typical technology timeline (inspired by PBS).

In Figure 2-4, you can find a single blip in the 1980s representing when the personal computer (PC) came into existence. Sitting there, it looks entirely polite and well behaved. You'll notice it doesn't take up more space than its neighbors, and it seems happy with its lot in life, perhaps sharing afternoon tea with its interesting friends the artificial heart and genetic engineering. But if we zoomed in, increasing the resolution so that the history of the PC

---

25 Ralph Nader's 1965 book, *Unsafe at Any Speed* (Grossman), revealed how collusion in the automotive industry prevented innovations in safety. See *http://www. answers.com/topic/unsafe-at-any-speed*.

was more than a single spot on a timeline, we'd see a chaotic, competitive, and unpredictable tangle of events. That happy little dot is a shill in the timeline's unavoidable deception. Not only do timelines express a false omnipotent view of history, they're superficial, offering an illusion of comprehensiveness. History is deep, and, like a fractal, you can find much to see at different layers. Let's dig in and see where that little dot for the PC goes.

When the development of the PC began in the late '70s, there were many possibilities for how (and even if) it would be delivered to the world. Mainframes were the dominant design, and only a curious minority believed computers would be in people's offices, much less their homes. Apple Inc.'s 1977 release of the Apple II computer is credited with proving that there was a viable market for personal computers. However, Xerox PARC (a research institute at the copier company) developed an earlier personal computer, the Alto, in 1973. The door for the Apple II's success was opened when two things happened. First, two leading companies, Atari and Hewlett-Packard, rejected Apple's proposal to manufacture its computer for them.[26] Second, Xerox chose not to market the Alto, despite having plans in hand. Both facts seem stupid today, but that's hindsight talking; at the time, Atari, Xerox, and HP made reasonable business decisions.

If you made a rough sketch of the possibilities of personal computing in 1980, you'd have something like Figure 2-5. Unlike the timeline in Figure 2-4, the graph shows how many different possible simultaneous directions were pursued, each one challenging, inspiring, and feeding off the others. But the timeline hides all this action—the juicy chaotic details innovators need to understand.

And since the timeline must show a single date for the PC, the year 1983 was chosen: not 1973 (Alto), 1977 (Apple II), or 1979 (Atari 400). In 1982, the PC was popular enough for *Time* to name it "Man of the Year" (suggesting, perhaps, that I could run for gadget of the decade, though I suspect I won't be asked), but it was later on, around 1983, that the IBM PC was the true dominant design. The dot on the timeline is an amazing averaging of knowledge: it can't even hint at when the idea of the personal computer was first explored, or at the struggles the unnamed pioneers

---

[26] *http://www.islandnet.com/~kpolsson/comphist/.*

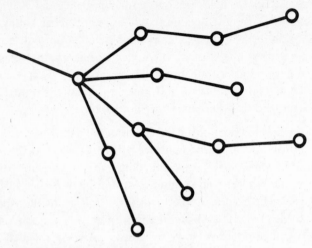

Figure 2-5. *The tree of competing innovations.*

of innovation had to overcome with electricity, mathematics, and transistors to pave the way for Apple, Atari, and IBM to finish things off decades later.[27] While the IBM PC did become the dominant design, we have to be careful about drawing conclusions about why. It was never preordained, nor did it come solely because of IBM's monopolistic dominance (they would release the comically stillborn PCjr soon after).[28] It's worth considering what would have happened if Xerox had chosen to release its Alto, or if Apple had convinced Hewlett-Packard to bankroll its machine: IBM would not have had the same opportunity. In the other direction, had Xerox or IBM taken risks earlier, the PC timeline might have shifted forward, but without lessons learned from watching competitors, it's possible that their immature products—launched before the technology or the culture was ready—could have set back the timeline until 1985 or even 2005 (see Figure 2-6).

Many innovations, such as the development of the web browser almost 20 years after the PC, follow similar patterns of innovation. The first popular web browser was NCSA's Mosaic, released in 1993 for the Windows operating system (the dominant-design OS for the dominant-design IBM PC). Within two years, there

---

[27] A better, though still simple, timeline of the events that led to the personal computer can be found at *http://inventors.about.com/library/blcoindex.htm.*

[28] *http://www.old-computers.com/museum/computer.asp?c=186.*

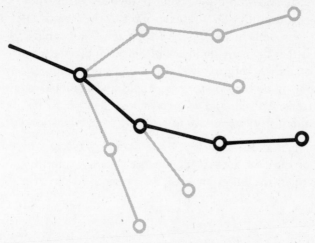

Figure 2-6. At best, timelines show only one path of the full tree of innovation history.

were more than a dozen competitors in the browser market; by 1997, the count was over 40.[29] In those early years, browsers were so prolific that other software, like word processors or games, often included a web browser made by that company. By 1997, two dominant players remained, Netscape Navigator and Microsoft Internet Explorer (disclosure: I worked on this product from 1994–1999), and they competed in what was grandly named "the browser wars," with Internet Explorer becoming the dominant design by 1999. Few alternatives were popular until 2005 when the release of Mozilla Firefox—a reinvention of Netscape Navigator—started a new wave of interest and innovation in browser competition, which has continued to accelerate even today. At this level of detail, there are many interesting questions. Why didn't the browser wars last longer? Did those years of intense competition work in the best interest of consumers, or are there more opportunities now that there's an aging dominant design in place for browsers like Firefox, Google's Chrome, or whatever comes next, to take larger risks and push another wave of innovation forward? And on it goes. The history behind personal

---

[29] A concise history of web browsers can be found at *http://www.livinginternet.com/wiwi_browse.htm*. For a deeper history of the hypertext systems web browsers were born from, see Jakob Nielsen, *Multimedia and Hypertext: The Internet and Beyond* (Morgan Kaufmann, 1995).

computers and web browsers alone involves many books' worth of stories, decisions, inspirations, and surprises impossible to represent here, much less in one happy timeline-bound dot.[30] My point is that there are hundreds of similar dots on any timeline, at any scale, each with its own fascinating stories and lessons. You can zoom in on the story of, say, Apple, and again on any product or person involved, and find an entirely new set of insights and inspirations (try *http://www.folklore.org* for a fantastic start).

But enough about history: it's one thing to explore why innovations of the past grew to dominance, but it's something else to innovate in the uncertainty of the present, which we'll explore next.

---

[30] For Xerox PARC, see Michael A. Hiltzik, *Dealers of Lightning: Xerox PARC and the Dawn of the Computer Age* (Collins, 2000); for Macintosh, see Steven Levy, *Insanely Great: The Life and Times of Macintosh, the Computer That Changed Everything* (Penguin, 2000); and for PCs generally, see Paul Freiberger and Michael Swaine, *Fire in the Valley: The Making of the Personal Computer* (McGraw-Hill, 2000).

CHAPTER 3

There is a method for innovation

By definition, innovation is a charge into the unknown.
—Unknown

Every Tuesday morning, Mr. K., my chemistry teacher, stumbled into the high school science lab, unlocked the chemistry cabinet, and built the most destructive science experiments known to man. He would repeat these pyrotechnic feats, ignoring scorched desks and terrified students, until he passed out or ran out of ammunition. After demanding that we replicate his chemical prowess, he'd storm out of the room, rarely seen until the following week. I haven't lost my fear of Bunsen burners and glass vials, but I remember one concept important to all innovative pursuits that those experiments etched into my mind: methodology (see Figure 3-1).

Figure 3-1. A science teacher demonstrating the concept of methodology.

A method, as defined by the *American Heritage Dictionary*, is a systematic way of accomplishing something. I deduced from Mr. K.'s behavior in class that no matter how late a person was out on a given night, or how many bars he visited before sleeping in his car, if he faithfully followed the methodological formulas of chemistry, he could achieve the same results repeatedly without risk. Despite threats to the contrary, no students were ever harmed in his presence. The immutable laws of science, Mr. K. proclaimed, are all powerful, as they have a consistency beyond everything known to man.

But life is larger than science. What we want in life is more complex than what can be achieved by mixing smelly powders or dropping Mentos into large bottles of Diet Coke (do try this, but do it outside).[1] And unlike school assignments, we don't want the same results every time. To innovate is to make something new, and progressive science—the discovery of knowledge—is a far cry from what went on in Mr. K.'s lab. A true experiment has at least one unknown variable, and the experiment is to see how that variable, well, varies. What happens if you juggle magnetized bowling balls under water or deep-fry a sack of Twinkies in space? If no one knows for certain, you have an experiment on your hands.

While it's one thing to come up with a new idea, and a second to try it out and see how it works, it's a less-interesting third to follow safe, well-practiced instructions that someone—perhaps a pyromaniac teacher—has laid out for you. Real experiments have risks, just like real life: consider Marie Curie, who discovered radiation but died from it, or the millions of lab rats put out of their cheesy misery every year in the name of exploring new ideas. Innovating comes at a price: it might be money, time, sanity, friends, or marriages, but there will definitely be one.

The myth of methodology, in short form, is the belief that a playbook exists for innovation and, like Mr. K.'s deceptively quaint instructions, it removes risk from the process of finding new ideas. It's the same wish that fuels secret lusts for time-saving gadgets, tasty but low-fat meals (ha), and five-step programs for <insert problem here>. And like other myths, this fantasy sells faster than truth, explaining the films, novels, and infomercials that play on it.

---

1 *http://eepybird.com/dcm1.html.*

But from experience, clarity, and hindsight, we know the *impos* sible never happens. We know it's not called the *if-you're-lucky-* possible or the *if-you-read-a-fancy-book-it-may-work*-possible for good reason. There is no way to avoid all risks when doing new things. It takes resources to start a company, develop an idea, or even change someone's mind, and those investments have no guaranteed returns. Even the scientific method, the process behind the ubiquitous "rocket science," doesn't promise success—consider the *Apollo 13* mission or the *Challenger* space shuttle disaster. And methods created by gurus or famous executives fall well short of predictive; all the greatest innovators in history experienced more failures than successes. While there is good advice to be found in these methods and stories, it's a far cry from methodology.

Faith in the myth of methodology, or in anything at all, can inspire people to overcome their fears. But don't confuse inspiration with execution—passion and confidence are fuel for work, but they don't guarantee success.

How innovations start

The top question famed innovators hear is "How did you start?" It's the beginnings that drive our curiosity: when did Edison get the idea for the lightbulb, or how did the Google founders envision a better search engine? Everyone wants to know where the magic happened, and since they can't imagine the magic sprinkled across years of work, they assume it's a secret—a tangible, singular element hiding behind the start. Like our endless quest to explain the origins of things, we're prone to seeking magic in beginnings.

It's this desire that leads otherwise bright minds to research Michael Jordan's breakfast, da Vinci's or Einstein's napping habits, or Linus Torvalds' (founder of Linux) chosen style of underwear.[2] The irrelevance of these details is obvious here in the logical confines of this book, but we've all considered similarly ridiculous questions about someone we admire. I once researched which typewriter Hemingway had and which inks Shakespeare used to pen his plays. Dreams don't run on logic: when we follow

---

2 I don't know what kind of underwear Linus wears, but my guess is he goes commando: *http://en.wikipedia.org/wiki/Linus_Torvalds*.

our emotions, we find both amazing and ridiculous things, and it takes time to sort one from the other, or to realize they are one and the same.

The eventual problem with excessive, dreamy curiosity is that—instead of making our own beginnings, right here and now—we seek to reuse others' proven magic. We try to borrow their beginnings and retrofit them into our lives.[3] Of course, still safe in this book, we know details from others' experiences are unlikely to be pivotal in our own—what worked for them, during their era, won't necessarily work for anyone else. For example, imagine that Alexander the Great was born in Iceland or Steve Jobs in medieval France—how well would their "magic" work in those environments? There are countless factors in any success story, and only some belong to the innovators as individuals.

Bo Peabody, venture capitalist and founder of Tripod (the eighth largest website in 1998) wrote, "Luck is a part of life, and everybody, at one point or another, gets lucky. But luck is a big part of business life and perhaps the biggest part of entrepreneurial life."[4] Acknowledging the uncontrollable factors helps divorce us from worshiping the details of our heroes' achievements. Studying history grants power, but only when we overcome romance and see innovators as humans just like us with similar limitations and circumstantial influences.

The best advice I've read on starting creative work comes from John Cage, often considered the most innovative composer of the 20th century,[5] who said, "It doesn't matter where you start, as long as you start." He meant that there can be no perfect beginning: it's only after you start—no matter how roughly—that you

---

[3] "Until one is committed, there is hesitancy, the chance to draw back—Concerning all acts of initiative (and creation), there is one elementary truth that ignorance of which kills countless ideas and splendid plans: that the moment one definitely commits oneself, then Providence moves, too. All sorts of things occur to help one that would never otherwise have occurred. A whole stream of events issues from the decision, raising in one's favor all manner of unforeseen incidents and meetings and material assistance, which no man could have dreamed would have come his way. Whatever you can do, or dream you can do, begin it. Boldness has genius, power, and magic in it. Begin it now." This quote is often misattributed to Goethe, but it's actually from *The Scottish Himalayan Expedition* by William Hutchinson Murray (*http://german.about.com/library/blgermyth12.htm*).

[4] Bo Peabody, *Lucky or Smart* (Random House, 2004).

[5] *http://en.wikipedia.org/wiki/John_Cage*.

can evaluate and build on what you've done, shift directions, or start over with the insight and perspective you've gained in the process. Innovation is best compared to exploration, and like Magellan or Captain Cook, you can't find something new if you limit your travels to places others have already found.

The seeds of innovation

The clichés about beginnings are true. The history of innovation is large enough that all the sayings, from Plato's famous "Necessity is the mother of invention" to Emerson's "Build a better mouse-trap and the world will beat a path to your door," hold some truth.[6] The trap, and the myth, is that evidence supporting one claim doesn't mean there isn't equally good evidence supporting another. Invention, and innovation, have many parents: the Taj Mahal (Figure 3-2) was built out of sorrow, the Babylonian Gardens were designed out of love,[7] the Empire State Building was constructed for ego, and the Brooklyn Bridge was motivated by pride. Name an emotion, motivation, or situation, and you'll find an innovation somewhere that it seeded.

However, it's simplifying and inspiring to categorize how things begin. While I've been very critical on the idea of a methodology for innovation in this chapter, there are patterns and frameworks than can be useful. I just think of them more as scaffolding—lightweight things that can be torn down and rearranged—rather than foundations. In reading the stories behind hundreds of innovations, I do see some patterns for how innovations begin, and they're captured here in six categories.

Hard work in a specific direction

The majority of innovations come from dedicated people in a field working hard to solve a well-defined problem. It's not sexy, and it won't be in any major motion pictures anytime soon, but it's the truth. Their starts are ordinary: in the cases of DNA (Watson and Crick), Google (Page and Brin), and the computer

---

6 We'll see in Chapter 8 that Emerson probably never said this.

7 The Babylonian Gardens are a disputed entry in the Seven Wonders of the World because they may never have existed: *http://ancienthistory.suite101.com/article.cfm/the_hanging_gardens_of_babylon*.

Figure 3-2. Constructing the Taj Mahal required several innovations, all inspired by an emperor's sadness over his deceased wife.

mouse (Englebart), the innovators spent time framing the problem, enumerating possible solutions, and then began experimenting. Similar tales can be found in the origins of the developments of television (Farnsworth)[8] and cell phones (Cooper). Often, hard work extends for years. It took Carlson, the inventor of the photocopier, decades of concentrated effort before Xerox released its first copy machine.[9]

Hard work with direction change

Many innovations start in the same way as mentioned previously, but an unexpected opportunity emerges and is pursued midway through the work. In the classic tale of Post-it Notes, Art Fry at 3M unintentionally created weak glue, but he didn't just throw it away. Instead, he wondered: what might this be good for? For years he kept that glue around, periodically asking friends and colleagues whether it could be useful. Years later, he found a friend

---

[8] Singular inventorship is exceptionally rare, as we'll discuss in Chapter 5. For all of these innovations, others rightfully claim partial credit. Several books have been written on the history of television, and it's one of the most complex and distributed stories of innovation in the 20th century.

[9] *http://www.invent.org/hall_of_fame/27.html.*

who desired sticky paper for his music notations, giving birth to Post-it Notes. Teflon (a mechanical lubricant), tea bags (first used as packaging for loose tea samples), and microwaves (unexpected discharge from a radar system) all have similar origination stories. What's ignored is that the supposed "accident" was made possible by hard work and persistence, and it wouldn't have otherwise happened by waiting around.

Curiosity

Many innovations begin with bright minds following their personal interests. The ambition is to pass time, learn something new, or have fun. At some point, the idea of a practical purpose arises, commitments are made, and the rest is history. George de Mestral invented Velcro in response to the burrs he found on his clothes after a hike. He was curious about how the burrs stuck, put them under a microscope, and did some experiments. Like da Vinci, he found inspiration in the natural world, and he designed Velcro based on the interlocking hooks and loops of the burrs and his clothing (looking to nature for patterns to reuse is called *biomimicry*). Linus Torvalds began Linux as a hobby: a way to learn about software and explore making some of his own.[10] Much like the direction-change scenario, at some point, a possible use is found for the product of curiosity, and a choice is made to pursue it or follow curiosity elsewhere.

Wealth and money

Many innovations are driven by the quest for cash. Peter Drucker believed Thomas Edison's primary ambition was to be a captain of industry, not an innovator: "His real ambition...was to be a business builder and to become a tycoon."[11] Drucker also explains that Edison was a disaster in business matters, but that his profile was so prominent that—despite his entrepreneurial failures—his management methods are emulated today, particularly in Silicon Valley and venture capital firms.

---

[10] *http://www.redhat.com/docs/manuals/linux/RHL-6.2-Manual/getting-started-guide/.*

[11] From *Innovation and Entrepreneurship*, 13.

With half an innovation in hand, ideas but no product, it's natural to try to sell those ideas: let someone else take the risks of complete innovation. Instead of idealistic goals of revolution or changing the world, the focus is on reaping financial rewards without the uncertainties of bringing the ideas all the way to fruition. The Internet boom and bust of the 1990s was driven by start-up firms innovating, or pretending to innovate, just enough for established corporations to acquire them. In many cases, the start-ups imploded before acquisition or were acquired only for their ideas to be abandoned by the corporations' larger and conservative business plans.

The founders of many great companies initially planned to sell their ideas and designs to larger corporations but, unable to sell, reluctantly chose to go it alone. Google tried to sell to Yahoo! and AltaVista, Apple to HP and Atari, and Carlson (photocopier inventor) to nearly every corporation he could find.

Necessity

Waves of innovation have come from individuals in need of something they couldn't find. Craig Newmark, founder of Craigslist.org, needed a way to keep in touch with friends about local events. The simple email list grew too popular to manage and evolved into the website known today. Similarly, the founders of McDonald's developed a system for fast food production to simplify the management of their local homespun hamburger stand (Ray Kroc bought the company later and developed it into a multinational brand). Innovations that change the world often begin with humble aspirations.

Combination

Most innovations involve many factors, and it's daft to isolate one above others. Imagine an innovation that starts with curiosity and leads to hard work, but then the innovator's quest for wealth forces a direction change. Midway through, this direction change is interrupted by a stroke of good luck (say, winning the lottery), allowing the innovator to return to the initial direction with renewed perspective and motivation. The removal of any of those seeds from the story might end it—or might not. In many of the stories of innovation, we have to wonder: if the first "magical" event didn't take place, might the innovator have found a different seed instead? No matter what seeds are involved, all ideas overcome similar challenges, and studying them reveals as much as or more than the beginnings of innovation.

The challenges of innovation

Steve Jobs, founder of Apple and Pixar, was asked, "How do you systematize innovation?" (a common question among CEOs and the business community). His answer was, "You don't."[12] This was not what readers of *Business Week* expected, but foolish questions often receive disappointing answers. It's nearly as absurd a question as asking how to control weather or herd cats, because those approximate the lack of control and number of variables inherent in innovation. Jobs, or any CEO, might have a system for *trying* to manage innovation, or a *strategy* for managing the risks of new ideas, but that's a far cry from systematizing something (as even the legendary Jobs' failures with the Apple Lisa, NeXT computing, and the Macintosh portable indicate[13]). I wouldn't call anything with a 50% or worse failure rate a system, would you? The Boeing 777 has jet engines engineered for guaranteed 99.99% reliability—now that's a system and a methodology. It's true that innovation is riskier than engineering, but that doesn't mean we should use words like system, control, or process so casually.

A better question, one with useful answers, is: what challenges do innovations face? While success is unpredictable, the challenges can be identified and used as excellent tools. Any successful innovation can be studied for how those challenges were overcome, and any innovation in progress can be managed with those challenges in mind.

In this chapter's second swoop through the innovations of all time, I've categorized the eight challenges innovators confront.

---

12 *http://www.businessweek.com/magazine/content/04_41/b3903408.htm.*

13 *http://www.networkworld.com/community/node/44206?ap1=rcb.*

1. **Finding an idea.** Ideas can come from anywhere: concentrated thinking, daydreaming, personal problems, observations of others, a coincidence, or the result of studying something in the world (see Chapter 6). The idea could be for a problem you want to solve or merely for an experiment you want to follow (hoping the problem it solves will surface later—a scenario often mocked as a "solution in search of a problem").

2. **Developing a solution.** The idea is one thing; a working solution is another. Leonardo da Vinci sketched a helicopter in the 1500s, but it would be centuries before developments in aerodynamics and engines would make even a working prototype possible. Execution demands more effort than idea generation, and it's difficult to know how much more until you try. When developing something new, technologies, bank accounts, and people all have a surprising tendency to disappoint, sending humbled innovators back for variations of challenge #1: many smaller ideas need to be found to enable the big idea. Or, the idea is narrowed to make development possible.

3. **Sponsorship and funding.** How will you fund the project, including #2? If you work for someone else, you'll need permission or political influence. The management of innovation—in an MBA sense—is finding, working with, and satisfying sponsors, or positioning an innovation within their political climate and objectives. If you're independent, you'll need investors or bank loans, and you must complete enough of #2 to convince them you're worthy of their support.

4. **Reproduction.** It's difficult to scale something: you might design a better mousetrap, but can you manufacture 50,000 cheaply enough to profit? It's a different challenge to make thousands of something than it is to make one. Software and new technologies are appealing to innovators because they ease many reproduction challenges (DVDs are cheap to reproduce, as are websites or servers), but they face issues of scale: having enough bandwidth, speed, or services to satisfy customers. Cheap reproduction also creates "noise": low expenses mean the numbers of competitors can be large, making it hard for customers to find you.

5. **Reaching potential customers.** An idea is not an innovation until it reaches people. Some trivialize this by saying they "don't do marketing," but the truth is that many innovations fail because they never reach the people they're designed for. Great innovations have been lost for decades, recovered only when someone found a way to bring them to the right people. The wheel, the steam engine, and freeze-dried foods were innovations that existed before 100 BCE, but it took centuries for innovators to position each of them in ways the average person could use. *Lost Discoveries*, by Dick Teresi, details dozens of innovations lost to civilization for generations—failures of marketing and communication more so than of technology.

6. **Beating competitors.** While you're working hard at #1–5, you won't be alone. Steve Jobs (Apple) was not the only maker of personal computers. Bill Gates (Microsoft) did not have the only operating system. Jeff Bezos (Amazon.com) did not have the first online bookstore. The opportunity seen by every successful innovator is visible to others, and those who succeed always leave competitors in their wake. Every breakthrough, at any time, is chased by dozens of talented and motivated people—the wise innovator keeps an eye on her peers' work for purposes of collaboration, inspiration, or tactical recognizance.

7. **Timing.** As great as your idea is, will the culture be ready when it's finished? Revolutionary ideas can be too much change for people to handle. Innovations often need to be explained in terms of the status quo, which is why automobiles are rated in horsepower and electric lights in candles. The risk is that a sufficiently advanced idea, regardless of how it's positioned, won't match the interests or concerns of the moment. Timing is also a factor: what news will break on the day you announce your innovation? What components needed to finish your innovation are delivered late? What will other players and competitors do on the day you launch?

8. **Keeping the lights on.** While you're dealing with all the innovation fun above, the bills will keep coming. Being an innovator doesn't give you a "get out of other obligations free" card.

The probability of innovation

As a back-of-the-envelope sketch of innovation difficulty, let's assume there is a 50% chance of succeeding at each challenge (which, given the data, is generous). Because success at one challenge is dependent on success at the previous, the probability of overcoming all challenges is low:

$$50\% \times 50\% \times 50\% \times 50\% \times 50\% \times 50\% \times 50\% \times 50\% = .390625\%$$

That's less than 1%. Of course, if your innovation requires only convincing your friends to try a new poker variation, or your boss to run meetings differently, you might face two (and not all eight) challenges, and odds improve based on your skills, experience, and teammates. It's safe to say that the smaller the ambition, the better the odds. But dreams and passions, the saving throw against probability, might fade.[1] And, as Han Solo said, "Never tell me the odds."[2]

[1] *Saving throw* is a term from role-playing games, where a character has a certain percent chance, influenced by his talents or magic powers of avoiding nasty things. See *http://en.wikipedia.org/wiki/Saving_throw*.

[2] In *The Empire Strikes Back*, *http://imdb.com/title/tt0080684/quotes*.

The infinite paths of innovation

The good news that arises from all of these challenges is that there are many ways to succeed. We're lucky: all the great things civilization has created did happen, despite all the reasons they didn't have to. However, which paths are open or closed at any moment is impossible to know. The path that worked last week is not guaranteed to work today, and an innovation that has failed in the past might just be the right thing for right now. Successful innovations are highly unpredictable, even in the view of experts or the innovators themselves, as is the case of three unlikely but telling success stories: Flickr, 3M, and Craigslist.

Flickr

In the summer of 2002, a small team of Vancouver programmers were working to build an online game called *Game Neverending*. The idea was to build an experience so fun and interesting that people would pay money to spend time in this invented world (similar to today's popular and addictive *World of Warcraft*).

One goal the programmers had was to make communication easy between people inside the game, easier even than being in the same room. They built a simple tool that allowed players to talk, exchange instant messages, and share photos. It was a minor part of a major project and, at the time, not much was thought of it.

As weeks passed, they realized the photo-sharing tool they'd built was a more promising business than the game itself. It was fun to use, and as it was improved, it developed features that even professional photo-sharing tools didn't have. With the game incomplete, and their 2002 post-boom tech-sector financing running thin, they strapped on their seatbelts and changed direction. In 2003, the tool launched under the name Flickr and quickly found a following. Since Flickr's design wasn't nurtured under the scrutiny of a business model, it delivered higher-quality service to customers with ideas none of the existing competitors had ever thought to do. As Caterina Fake, one of Flickr's founders, commented, "Had we sat down and said, 'Let's start a photo application,' we would have failed."[14] Because they had the freedom to design a photo application without any constraints, they were able to design something unique. While Flickr itself probably never made a profit, its technology, design, and loyal customers were attractive enough for Yahoo! to purchase it—even though Yahoo! had its own photo-sharing service.

The folks at Flickr did two key things. First, they recognized the unexpected value of the photo tool. And second, they were willing to make big changes and reinvest everything in a different direction. The paradox is that the opportunity to do these two things presented itself in the course of doing something else: making a computer game. No methodology could guide someone in determining, in that moment, when to abandon one direction and reinvest in another. It is possible that, had they continued with the game, it would have been successful, and I'd be writing about the game in this book, instead of Flickr.

It's easy to find similar stories of "innovation by curious path." Today, Google is well known for its rule of giving employees 20% of work time for their own projects, hoping to inspire Flickr-esque innovations. But Google is far from the first company to offer this

---

[14] *http://www.usatoday.com/tech/products/2006-02-27-flickr_x.htm.*

kind of incentive. 3M, the well-known products conglomerate, began the practice of employee-chosen projects decades earlier, and their success is a great story of its own.

3M

3M started as Minnesota Mining and Manufacturing Co. in 1902, drilling underground for mineral deposits used to make grinding wheels: a most unexpected beginning for the future makers of cute yellow Post-it Notes. It took 15 years for the struggling company to post profits, mostly with their line of quality sandpaper. Then in 1925, Richard G. Drew, a lab assistant, needed a transparent way to mark borders on objects: namely, automobiles scheduled for two-tone paint jobs.[15] After some experimentation on his own time, masking tape was born, and the history of 3M was changed forever.[16] William McKnight, 3M's general manager, learned from Drew that innovation comes from the bottom where exploration happens; under his leadership, they developed a culture that supports mavericks and experimenters, explaining their amazing $20 billion in annual sales.[17]

Craigslist

One last path to innovation started in 1995 at the dawn of the Internet Age. Craig Newmark, a software engineer in San Francisco, wanted a way to exchange information with friends about cool events happening around his hometown.[18] At first he used email, but soon there was enough traffic that an email list was needed so people could post and reply without annoying each other. At the time, there were many commercial services for this sort of information, from newspapers to newsletters to community bulletin boards, but something about the informal and profitless ambitions of an email list made it a popular alternative. In 1997,

---

[15] *http://web.mit.edu/invent/iow/drew.html.*

[16] According to legend, prototypes of the tape failed so miserably that Drew was scolded, told to take his tape back to his Scotch (i.e., parsimonious) bosses, and put more adhesive on it. He kept the name, and Scotch tape was how the product was marketed.

[17] William McKnight captured his philosophy well in a speech given in 1948, summing up in three paragraphs a set of simple ideals modern managers rarely have the courage to live up to. See *http://www.answers.com/topic/william-l-mcknight.*

[18] *http://www.craigslist.org/about/craig_newmark.*

Craig formalized the noncommercial nature of the list, preferring to protect its authenticity and simplicity. It wasn't until 1999 that Craig decided to make Craigslist.org the focus of his working life. Today, the list is one of the most effective job-posting and community-building websites in the United States, and generates more revenue per employee than most major tech-sector companies ($100 million in 2010 revenue with 30 employees[19]), not to mention being a catalyst in putting some major American newspapers out of business. Had you rounded up all of the great innovation experts and authors from these times, none of them would have predicted these outcomes. In all three cases, common sense would have dictated that the markets involved (photo software, office products, and classified ads) were highly saturated businesses with few opportunities. But now, looking back (as we learned in Chapter 2), it seems inevitable that these markets were ripe for change.

Finding paths of innovation

While there are no maps, there are attitudes that help. Any good survival training course teaches not just skills, but ways to think. The comparison between innovation and survival is apt; to follow the comparison, here are ways of thinking about paths that can shift the odds.

- **Gain self-knowledge.** Every tough decision is made in part by how the innovator feels about herself: none of us is as logical as we like to believe. Being aware of the environments or challenges that inspire the best results for your personality helps you make smart path choices. The best business opportunity might be the least interesting personal challenge, and vice versa. Knowing yourself, and your team, is a big advantage and should guide decisions. It's one of the few uncertainties of innovation that, given time, can always be converted into certain knowledge and used as an asset.

- **Reward interesting failures.** If you are exploring the unknown, failures will happen. Having a positive attitude about failure is therefore critical (which isn't to say making

---

[19] http://37signals.com/svn/posts/2283-ranking-tech-companies-by-revenue-per-employee.

stupid mistakes should be encouraged). But any mistake that teaches you, or someone who works with you, something previously unknowable without having done the experiment is a valuable lesson. And it's this attitude that is consistent among all great inventors. They rewarded themselves for doing experiments and learning from them, rather than exclusively rewarding success.

• **Be intense, but step back.** Many successful innovators work passionately, but periodically step back and ask, "What is happening in the world that impacts my goals?" or "What else is my work good for?" Innovation is powered by the combination of intensity and a willingness to reconsider assumptions, minimizing the chance of following dead ends and maximizing the potential for finding better paths. Honest friends can lend their perspectives if asked—you just have to be ready to hear hard truths. It's difficult to bet years on an idea and maintain the courage to question, rethink, and fully commit again in a different direction.

• **Grow to size.** No patent was written and filed in an hour, and no symphony was orchestrated overnight. Changing the world or revolutionizing an industry is a nice fantasy, but it's foolish to start with those ambitions because they're out of any individual's control. All things equal, it makes more sense to attack a specific problem in a known field; only as successes accrue should the ambition grow. Many world-changing ideas had humble beginnings and started with small questions like, "Can I make this better?" Use ego and ambition to fuel a progression of innovations and not to distract you from the best opportunities, however ordinary, nearby.

• **Honor luck and the past.** The great egos of innovation have one success story that they repeat (to the misery of their companions) forever. Never having the courage to attempt something new or admit the role of luck, they spend much of the present talking about the past. Honoring luck doesn't diminish an accomplishment: it's an acknowledgment to others that you can do everything right and fail, and do many things wrong and succeed. The greatest innovators never failed to acknowledge luck, chance, and the sacrifices of their predecessors. Isaac Newton wrote, "I have stood on the shoulders of giants,"[20] and Einstein noted, "Anyone who has never made a mistake has never tried anything new." Perhaps innovators deserve the most respect for their courage in confronting uncertainty, a fear common to us all.

---

[20] This quote was almost certainly false modesty. Newton was arrogant, often resorting to childish mockery of his many adversaries.

CHAPTER 4

People love new ideas

Imagine it's 1874, and you've just invented the telephone. After high-fiving your friend Watson, you head down to Western Union—the greatest communication company in the world—and show your work. Despite your excellent pitch (a century before PowerPoint), Western Union turns you down on the spot, calls the telephone a useless toy, and shows you to the door. Would you have given up? What if the next five companies turned you down? The next 25? How long would it take you to lose faith in your ideas?

Fortunately, Alexander Graham Bell, the telephone's inventor, didn't listen to the folks at Western Union.[1] He started his own business and changed the world, paving the way for the mobile phone in your pocket. Similar stories surround innovators like Google founders Larry Page and Sergey Brin, whose page rank ideas were turned down by AltaVista and Yahoo!, the dominant search companies of the day. George Lucas was told all kinds of no by every major Hollywood studio but one, for the original *Star Wars* screenplay. And, don't forget that Einstein's $E=mc^2$, Galileo's sun-centered solar system, and Darwin's theory of evolution were laughed at for years by experts around the world.

Every great idea in history has the big, red stamp of rejection on its face. It's hard to see today because once ideas gain acceptance, we gloss over the hard paths they took to get there. If you scratch any innovation's surface, you'll find the scars: they've been roughed up and thrashed around—by both the masses and leading minds—before they made it into your life. Paul C. Lauterbur, winner of the Nobel Prize for coinventing MRI, explained, "You can write the entire history of science in the last 50 years in terms of papers rejected by *Science* or *Nature*."[2] Big ideas in all fields endure dismissals, mockeries, and persecutions (of them and their creators) on their way to changing the world. Many novels in classics libraries, including James Joyce's *Ulysses*, Mark Twain's *The Adventures of Huckleberry Finn*, and J. D. Salinger's *The Catcher*

---

[1] Bell is often credited as the inventor, but as you'll learn in Chapter 5, it's rarely that simple. Elisha Gray, Philipp Reis, Innocenzo Manzetti, and others have similar claims. For a chronology of inventors who possibly contributed to the telephone, see *http://en.wikipedia.org/wiki/Invention_of_the_telephone*. And while Western Union did reject Bell's proposal, it's unclear how strong their rejection was. (If they saw its potential, would it have been wise to tell Bell on the spot?)

[2] Kevin Davies, "Public Library of Science Opens Its Doors," *BIO-IT World* (February 2007), *http://www.bio-itworld.com/archive/111403/plos/*.

in the Rye were banned upon publication; great minds like Socrates and Plato even rejected the idea of books at all.[3]

The love of new ideas is a myth: we prefer ideas only after others have tested them. We confuse truly new ideas with good ideas that have already been proven, which just happen to be new to us. Even innovators themselves read movie reviews, consult Zagat restaurant ratings, and shop at IKEA, distributing the burden of dealing with new ideas. How did you choose your apartment, your beliefs, or even this book? We reuse ideas and opinions all the time, rarely committing to the truly *new*. But we should be proud; it's smart. Why not recycle good ideas and information? Why not take advantage of the conclusions other people have made to efficiently separate what's good and safe from what's bad and dangerous? Innovation is expensive: no one wants to pay the price for ideas that turn out to be not quite ready for prime time.

There is an evolutionary advantage in this fear of new things. Any ancestor who compulsively jumped off every newly discovered cliff or ate only scary-looking plants died off quickly. We happily let brave souls like Magellan, Galileo, and Neil Armstrong take intellectual and physical risks on our behalf, watching from a safe distance, following behind (or staying away) once we know the results. Innovators are the test pilots of life, taking big chances so we don't have to. Even early adopters, people who thrive on using the latest things, are at best adventurous consumers, not creators. They rarely take the same risks on unproven ideas as the innovators themselves.

The secret tragedy of innovators is that their desire to improve the world is rarely matched by support from those they hope to help.

Managing the fears of innovation

What's the most stressful thing that can happen to you? Juggling hungry cocaine-addicted baby tigers? Doing stand-up comedy in front of your coworkers and in-laws? Well, if you believe the studies, it's the big five: divorce, marriage, moving, death of a loved one, and getting fired.[4] All stressful events, including tiger-juggling,

---

3 Plato, *Phaedrus*, *http://classics.mit.edu/Plato/phaedrus.html*. In this dialogue, the risks of using books—instead of spoken language—are debated. They feared people would become stupid if they adopted the technology of writing; similar fears arise with every new technology.

4 *http://www.surgeongeneral.gov/library/mentalhealth/chapter4/sec1_1.html*.

combine fear of suffering with forced change. A divorce or new job demands that your life change in ways out of your control, triggering instinctive fears: if you don't do something clever soon, you're going to be miserable (or dead). Although it's possible to endure the big five simultaneously, a notion that quiets most complaints about life, surviving just one devastates most people for months.

Now imagine some relaxing events: reading a funny novel by the ocean or having beers with friends by a midnight campfire. They're activities with little risk and guaranteed rewards. We've done these things many times and know that others have done them successfully and happily in the past. These are the moments we wish we had more of. We work hard so we can maximize the amount of time spent on the planet doing these kinds of things.

Innovation conflicts with this desire. It asks for faith in something unknown over something known to be safe, or even pleasant. A truly innovative Thanksgiving turkey recipe or highway driving technique cannot be risk-free. Whatever improvement it might yield is uncertain the moment it is first tried (or however many attempts are needed to get it right). No matter how amazing an idea is, until proven otherwise, its imagined benefits will pale in comparison to the real, and unimagined, fear of change.

This creates an unfortunate paradox: the greater the potential of an idea, the harder it is to find anyone willing to try it (more on this in Chapter 8). For example, solutions for world peace and world hunger might be out there, but human nature makes it difficult to attempt them. The bigger the changes needed to adopt an innovation, the more fears rise.

> *There is nothing more difficult to take in hand, more perilous to conduct, or more uncertain in its success, than to take the lead in the introduction of a new order of things. For the reformer has enemies in all those who profit by the old order, and only lukewarm defenders in all those who would profit by the new order, this lukewarmness arising partly from fear of their adversaries...and partly from the incredulity of mankind, who do not truly believe in anything new until they have had actual experience of it.*
> —Niccolo Machiavelli

Negative things innovators hear

Every creator hears similar criticisms to his ideas. While I don't have proof, I bet the first caveman who captured fire, the first Sumerian with a wheel, the first person to do anything interesting in any society in human history, heard one of the following after pitching his idea:

- This will never work.
- No one will want this.
- It can't work in practice.
- People won't understand it.
- This isn't a problem.
- This is a problem, but no one cares.
- This is a problem and people care, but it's already solved.
- This is a problem, and people care, but it will never make money.
- This is a solution in search of a problem.
- Get out of my office/cave now.

Sometimes very smart people say these things. Ken Olsen, founder of the Digital Equipment Corporation, said in 1977, "There is no reason anyone would want a computer in their home." The leading art critics in France, in response to the opening of the Eiffel Tower, made comments like, "[That] tragic lamp post springing up from its bowels...[is] like a beacon of disaster and despair."5 It took the British Navy, at the peak of their dominance in the 17th century, 150 years to adopt a proven remedy for scurvy.

Bo Peabody, serial entrepreneur, writes, "It's astounding the number of people who will tell you that you and your ideas are crazy. I have been thrown out of more than a thousand offices while building my six companies."6 Remember, it's hard to know the future, and all great minds have failed to predict what would take off and what wouldn't. My point isn't to make fun of famous

---

5 Olsen's quote is disputed by some, who claim he was for personal computers, but simply didn't see them running people's homes like they do on *Star Trek*. The quote on Eiffel's work is retold in John H. Lienhard, *The Engines of Our Ingenuity* (Oxford University Press, 2006), 186.

6 From *Lucky or Smart*, 28.

people for being wrong; instead, it's to point out that we're all wrong much of the time (see Figure 4-1).

Figure 4-1. Many critics demanded that the Eiffel Tower be torn down when it was built. Today, it's one of the most popular attractions in Paris.

Experienced innovators anticipate these criticisms. They prepare refutations or preempt them, as in, "Who would want electricity in their homes? Let me tell you who..."[7] But even with preparation,

---

7 Edison was a shameless promoter of electricity, crossing moral and ethical lines. He created the first electric chair to demonstrate that his competitors' designs were unsafe, unlike his (which wasn't true). Matthew Josephson, *Edison: A Biography* (McGraw-Hill, 1959), 348–349.

charm, and amazing ideas, convincing people to see an idea in the same way its creator sees it is difficult. Most have little interest in having their minds changed, something that's hard to remember when you've spent your life savings, or an entire weekend, killing yourself to invent something. This gap—the difference between how an innovator sees her work from how it's seen by others—is the most frustrating challenge innovators face. Creators expect to be well received. They look at accepted innovations and the heroes who delivered them and assume their new innovations will be treated the same way (see Figure 4-2). But no matter how brilliant an idea is, the gap exists. Until the innovation is accepted, it will be questioned relentlessly.

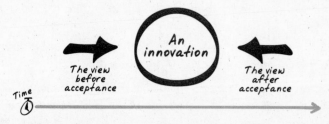

Figure 4-2. Innovators know of other innovations only after the fact, and they are surprised when their ideas are treated differently from the accepted innovations of the past.

Many innovators give up when they learn ideas—even with dazzling prototypes or plans in hand—are only the beginning. The challenges that follow demand skills of persuasion more than brilliance. As Howard H. Aiken, a famous inventor, said, "Don't worry about people stealing your ideas. If your ideas are any good, you'll have to ram them down people's throats."[8] Although beating up people to convince them rarely works, Aiken's point holds: people are unlikely to be as interested in your ideas as you are.

The observation many would-be innovators never make is that most criticisms are superficial. The spoken questions only hint at the real concerns. Responding to superficial comments is a loser's game; persuading demands mapping criticisms to deeper issues.

---

[8] *http://en.wikiquote.org/wiki/Howard_H._Aiken.*

All of the negative comments listed earlier can be mapped to one or more of the following perspectives:

- **Ego/envy:** I can't accept this because I didn't think of it, or I think I'll look weak if I say yes.
- **Pride and politics:** This makes me look bad.
- **Personal:** I don't like you, so I will never support your idea.
- **Fear:** I'm afraid of change.
- **Priority:** I have 10 innovative proposals but resources for one.
- **Sloth:** I'm lazy, bored, and don't want to think or do more work.[9]
- **Security:** I may lose something I don't want to lose.
- **Greed:** I can make money or build an empire if I reject this idea.
- **Consistency:** This violates my deeply held principles (no matter how absurd, outdated, or ridiculous they are).

The effect of these feelings, whether justified or irrational, is the same. They're just as real in the mind of the person feeling them as anything else. If your boss feels threatened by a proposal—even if those reasons seem entirely paranoid or delusional to you—those feelings will define his behavior in response to new ideas. If those feelings are strong, it's easy for him to use the comments above to reject proposals for even the greatest ideas. If the innovator defends only the superficial and makes no attempt to persuade the deeper feelings to change, or find ways to recast the innovation so that those feelings become positive, she will fail to get the support she needs.

For example, when Galileo claimed the sun was the center of the solar system, he faced persecution from the Church and the Western world for reasons listed above. It wasn't the idea itself that caused the outrage—it was how that idea made them feel. They didn't care about what was at the center of the solar system. Galileo would have been in similar trouble had he suggested the earth rotated around a purple dragon or a half-eaten sandwich. They weren't upset about the details of his theory; they were

---

[9] Related quote: "Most people would rather die than think; in fact, they do so." —*Bertrand Russell*

angry that anyone would advocate a theory different from the one they believed in (of course, making fun of the Pope didn't help any).[10] It was the principle of the thing, as well as how it questioned their sense of order—two common reasons for rejecting ideas that have nothing to do with the idea itself.

This is the magic double-secret principle: innovative ideas are rarely rejected on their merits; they're rejected because of how they make people feel. If you forget people's concerns and feelings when you present an innovation, or neglect to understand their perspectives in your design, you're setting yourself up to fail.

The innovator's dilemma explained

Earlier, I asked you to imagine inventing the telephone. Did you like that? Well, you'll like this even more, as this scenario has a surprise ending.

Imagine it's 1851, and you're sick and tired of waiting for the Pony Express to deliver important messages. You happen to meet a Mr. Morse and buy into his idea for using copper wire to send instant messages over great distances. Your friends laugh, telling you to get a real job because wires are silly things for grown men to play with. At great financial risk, you build the first cross-country cables in the U.S., and they work, changing the world. Your organization thrives for years; the nation is communicating, for a price, over your cutting-edge digital communication network. Wealthy and famous, you soon find attractive people throwing themselves and their money at you. But you're not finished: in a fit of innovation, you create the first stock ticker in 1866, give the nation its first standardized time service, and revolutionize the financial world with money transfers—allowing people to send cash thousands of miles across the country in seconds.

In the middle of your glory, as your rise to innovation fame reaches untold heights, a young man visits you. He holds an odd machine in his hands. He claims it will replace everything, especially all the things you've struggled all your life to build. He's young, arrogant,

---

10 In short, when Galileo wrote *Dialogue Concerning the Two Chief World Systems*, he put quotes from Pope Urban VIII into the mouth of his character Simplicio, a fool who is ridiculed for rejecting heliocentrism. See James Reston, *Galileo: A Life* (Beard Books, 2000).

and dismissive of your achievements. How long would you listen before you threw a telegraph at him? Could you imagine, given all you'd built, that something as simple as his clunky wooden box would replace everything you know? Or would you have the guts to give up the innovations you'd made and put everything behind the unknown?

This challenge of mind is known as the *innovator's dilemma*. The face-off between Western Union and Alexander Graham Bell (dramatized but roughly accurate in my telling) has been played out for centuries, with the captains of one aging innovation protecting their work from the threat of emerging ideas. The concept is well described in Clayton M. Christensen's book *The Innovator's Dilemma*, which provides hearty business examples of faith in the past, blinding smart people from the innovations of the future.[11]

It's both a psychological and economical phenomenon: as people and companies age, they have more to lose. They're not willing to spend years chasing dreams or to endanger what they've worked so hard to build. Attitudes focused on security, risk aversion, and optimization of the status quo eventually become dominant positions, and even become organizational policy at companies that were once young, nimble, and innovative. For these reasons, it's rare in art, music, writing, business, and every single creative pursuit for innovators to sustain that role throughout their lives. It's not that their talent wanes, it's more that their interests change. Having succeeded, their strongest desire is not to find new ideas to conquer, but to protect the success they've already earned.

Frustration + innovation = entrepreneurship?

The last 30 years have seen an amazing wave of innovation at the intersection of technology and entrepreneurship.[12] Companies like Apple, Google, Microsoft, HP, and Yahoo! started as small groups who dismissed the well-worn path of convincing others

---

11 Clayton M. Christensen, *The Innovator's Dilemma* (Harvard Business School Press, 2003).

12 This power combo has been a phenomenon since the early days of the Industrial Revolution, when the first steam engines, factories, and mining systems were pioneered by entrepreneurial technologists. See Arnold Pacey, *The Maze of Ingenuity* (MIT Press, 1992).

and chose instead to realize ideas on their own. These start-up ventures were born out of the frustration of failing to make innovation happen in larger, established businesses. Had the founders of these companies found positive responses from corporations, history might be different. Frustration with people in power is a perennial complaint among creative minds: Michelangelo and da Vinci were infuriated by their employers' limited ambitions and their peers' conservative natures, in the same way creative people are today.[13]

Innovators rarely find support within mainstream organizations, and the same stubbornness that drives them to work on problems others ignore gives them the strength necessary to work alone. This explains the natural bond between breakthrough thinkers and new companies: innovative entrepreneurs not only have the passion for new ideas, they also have the conviction to make sacrifices that scare established companies.

The risks for an individual focusing 100% of his resources on a crazy idea are small: it's one life. But for an organization of 500 or 10,000 people, the risks of betting large on a new idea are high. Even if the idea pays off, the organization will be forced to change, causing fears and negative emotions to surface from everyone invested in the success of the previous big idea. Of course, some corporations are so large that they can take great risks: they can lose $20 million on an experiment and survive. But these efforts fail so often that it's possible that having less to lose works against innovation, compared to scrappy bootstrapped efforts led by people with everything at stake.

But as rosy as it sounds, the entrepreneur, whether he's wealthy or happily subsisting on ramen noodles,[14] must eventually convince one group of people—customers—of the merit of his ideas. And if he doesn't have enough money to support his new ideas, or his family refuses to eat canned chili for the third straight month, he'll need to

---

[13] However, the major difference between the 15th century and the present day is opportunity. In Europe back then, if you had an idea for a cathedral design or siege weapons (hot technologies of the day), you were dependent on the one organization that could afford your services: the Church. But software programmers in the late 20th century and beyond not only have many patrons, they have the means to build their dreams themselves.

[14] For a trifecta of innovation, see Tadashi Katoh and Akira Imai, *Project X—Nissin Cup Noodle* (Digital Manga Publishing, 2006). It's a great read—in graphic-novel form—of how the office staple of noodles-in-a-cup was invented.

convince a second group—investors. As far as we know, both groups are human beings (though some debate the DNA of venture capitalists) and have the same emotional responses listed previously.

How innovations gain adoption: the truth about ideas before their time

One frequent saying in innovation circles is that an idea is "ahead of its time." What a strange phrase. How can an idea be ahead of its time? How can anything be ahead of its time? It makes little sense. What people mean when they say this is one of two things: they think the idea is cool but not necessarily good, or they think someday in the future a similar idea will be popular. But it's faint praise. How often do the things we imagine in the future ever come to be? Personal rocketships? Cars that fly? Nuclear-powered everything? The odds of cool ideas from sci-fi movies gaining adoption are low, and it's not much of a compliment to have something labeled "ahead of its time."[15] People don't slave away on insanely difficult work, sacrificing the pleasures of life, with the singular hope that, on their deathbeds, after everything they've done has been ignored, they will be told they were "ahead of their time." To be told your idea is ahead of its time is typically innovation pity, not praise, unless that was your actual goal.

But more importantly for us, this phrase exposes myths about how innovations do gain adoption in the world. First, it assumes technology progresses in a straight line (as covered in Chapter 2). To be ahead of its time implies that an idea *has* a time, marked in red at the universal innovation headquarters, waiting for people to catch up to it: an entirely inaccurate, innovation-centric view of how people live.

In *Diffusion of Innovations*, Everett M. Rogers writes:

> *Many technologists think that advantageous innovations will sell themselves, that the obvious benefits of a new idea will be widely realized by potential adopters, and that the innovation will therefore diffuse rapidly. Unfortunately, this is very seldom the case. Most innovations in fact diffuse at a surprisingly slow rate.*[16]

---

15 Notice I said movies, not sci-fi books. Films are visual media and choose technologies that look good or have dramatic value, not necessarily things that solve important problems, have progressive value, or obey the laws of physics.

16 Everett M. Rogers, *Diffusion of Innovations* (Free Press, 2003), 7.

The book takes an anthropological approach to innovation, suggesting that new ideas spread at speeds determined by psychology and sociology, not the abstract merits of those new ideas. This explains the mysteries of great innovations that fail and bad ideas that prevail; there are more significant factors than the ones inventors focus on. Technological prowess matters less than we think in the diffusion of innovation.

Rogers identifies five factors that define how quickly innovations spread; they belong in every innovator's playbook. Roughly summarized and loosely interpreted, they include:

1. **Relative advantage.** What value does the new thing have compared to the old? This is perceived advantage, determined by the potential consumer of the innovation, not its makers. This makes it possible for a valueless innovation—from the creator's perspective—to gain acceptance, while more valuable ones do not. Perceived advantage is built on factors that include economics, prestige, convenience, fashion, and satisfaction.

2. **Compatibility.** How much effort is required to transition from the current thing to the innovation? If this cost is greater than the relative advantage, most people won't try the innovation. These costs include people's value systems, finances, habits, or personal beliefs. Rogers describes a Peruvian village that rejected the innovation of boiling water because of cultural beliefs that hot foods were only for sick people. You could argue all you wanted about the great benefits of boiling water, but if a religious or cultural belief forbids it, you're wasting your breath. Technological compatibility is only part of what makes an innovation spread: the innovation has to be compatible with habits, beliefs, values, and lifestyles.

3. **Complexity.** How much learning is required to apply the innovation? If a box of free, high-quality, infinite battery-life cell phones (and matching solar-powered cell towers) mysteriously appeared in 9th-century England, usage would stay at 0%, as the innovation requires a jump in complexity that would terrify people ("They're witches' eggs—burn them!"). The smaller the perceived conceptual gap, the higher the rate of acceptance.

4. **Trialability.** How easy is it to try the innovation? Tea bags were first used as giveaways so people could sample tea

without buying large tins, radically improving the trialability of brewed tea.[17] Samples, giveaways, and demonstrations are centuries-old techniques for making it risk-free to try new ideas. This is why Gap lets you try on clothes, and the Honda dealership lets anyone with a pulse test-drive a car. Many websites today have freemium services, where the basics cost nothing but you pay for extras. The easier it is to try, the faster innovations diffuse.

5. **Observability**. How visible are the results of the innovation? The more visible the perceived advantage, the faster the rate of adoption, especially within social groups. Fashion fads are a great example of highly observable innovations that have little value beyond their observability. Advertising fakes observability, as many ads show people using a product—for example, drinking a new brand of beer while all kinds of wonderful things are happening. Many technologies have limited observability, say, software device drivers, compared to physical products like mobile phones and trendy handbags, which are highly visible when socializing.

This list clarifies why the speed at which innovations spread is determined by factors that are often ignored by their creators. They grow so focused on creating things that they forget that those innovations are good only if people can use them. While there's a lot to be said for raising bars and pushing envelopes, breakthroughs happen for societies when innovations diffuse, not when they remain forever "ahead of their time."

This list is a scorecard for learning from past innovations, as well as a tool for improving diffusion of innovations in the present. The key is not to trivialize this list as bastardized marketing, as if these traits can be grafted to an innovation after it's finished, or simply pumped into sales literature and advertising (though those efforts rarely make the difference). Is it a successful innovation if it's purchased but ignored or bought and soon returned? A better way to think of the list is as attributes of the innovation itself.

And since these factors vary from culture to culture, some innovations gain acceptance in surprising ways. There is no uniformity in

---

17 Joel Levy, *Really Useful: The Origins of Everyday Things* (Firefly Books Ltd, 2002).

progress around the world; innovations may be adopted by one culture or nation decades before another. As writer William Gibson quipped, "The future is already here—it's just not evenly distributed."[18] And no innovation is immune; everything new passes through culture in unpredictable ways and, given the limits of human nature, always will.

---

[18] *http://en.wikipedia.org/wiki/William_Gibson.*

CHAPTER 5

The lone inventor

Who invented the electric light? No, it wasn't Thomas Edison. Two lesser-known inventors, Humphry Davy and Joseph Swan, both developed working electric lights well before Edison. Think Ford invented the automobile? Wrong again. Unfortunately, popular credit for major innovations isn't decided by historians: it's driven by markets, circumstance, and popularity, forces not bound by accuracy. Often, even historians have trouble sorting it out. Here's what the U.S. Library of Congress has to say on the subject, specific to the automobile:[1]

> This question [of who invented it] does not have a straightforward answer. The history of the automobile is very rich and dates back to the 15th century when Leonardo da Vinci was creating designs and models for transport vehicles. There are many different types of automobiles—steam, electric, and gasoline—as well as countless styles. Exactly who invented the automobile is a matter of opinion. If we had to give credit to one inventor, it would probably be Karl Benz from Germany. Many suggest that he created the first true automobile in 1885/1886.

If the librarians at the largest library in the world don't know for certain, how could we? There are similar complexities surrounding most innovations, from the first steam engines to personal computers or even airplanes (no, the Wright brothers didn't invent them[2]). As simple as it seems to be, the history of innovation is complicated. Most innovations are not the solid, tangible, independent things we imagine them to be. Each one is made up of threads and relationships that don't separate easily or yield simple answers.

For example, take the electric light. When Edison sat down to design the lightbulb, he was far from the first person to try. If several people were trying to make it work, who deserves the credit? Would it be enough to come up with the idea itself? Have a prototype? Would it matter how long the prototype stayed alight? How bright it burned? How many people witnessed it? How many bulbs were sold? Would it matter whether they cost $5,000,000

---

1 http://www.loc.gov/rr/scitech/mysteries/auto.html.

2 Bet that got you to look at the footnotes. The Wright brothers were first to demonstrate sustained powered flight of a certain distance. But balloons, kites, gliders, and some powered winged vehicles did fly before. More so, the Wright brothers were great researchers and students, learning from birds as well as their competitors. Fred C. Kelly, The Wright Brothers: A Biography (Dover, 1989).

per bulb or weighed 500,000 pounds? Depending on which question is seen as most important, different names surface as the rightful owner of the title "inventor." However, as folks at the U.S. Library of Congress suggest, there is no guidebook: the rules change from innovation to innovation. While there is some guidance for resolving these issues, before we get to explore them, things get worse.

Beyond the innovation itself, there is the problem of precedence: various invented light sources date back as far as 70,000 BCE. The idea of a lightbulb, a small portable object that gives light, is beyond ancient—it's older than the screw (500 BCE), the wheel (3000 BCE), and the sword (5000 BCE).[3] The inventors of torches, candles, and lamps through history are mostly unnamed, but they certainly contributed to Swan's, Davy's, and Edison's thinking[4] (not to mention proving to the world the value of being able to easily see the way to the bathroom after sunset). In similar fashion, websites derive layouts and graphic design techniques from newspapers, which are based on the early typographies of the printing press, and on it goes. All innovations today are bound to innovations of the past.

And if that's not enough, there are the people who developed the glassmaking techniques required for the bulbs, the copper mining and metal refinement processes for the filaments, and countless other forgotten creators of the tools, machines, and mathematics Edison and other innovators used. Certainly their anonymous contributions were essential to the innovation known as the lightbulb—remove them from the past, and in that same puff of history-changing smoke, the electric light we know disappears.

The answer to the previous list of questions is simple: Edison, Ford, and countless innovators are recognized as sole inventors for convenience. The histories we know depart from the truth for the simple reason that it makes them easier to remember.

---

3 It was difficult to find hard evidence about the origins of all three of these ancient inventions, so the truth is that we're not really sure when they were created. The best single reference on the origins of ancient innovations is *Ancient Inventions* by Peter James and Nick Thorpe (Ballantine Books, 1994).

4 A concise history can be found at *http://inventors.about.com/od/lstartinventions/a/lighting.htm*.

The convenience of lone inventors

The most common convenience is order of exposure. Most of the world first learned of the idea of electric lights and lightbulbs from Edison. No matter the actual history, in their knowledge, he was the deliverer of the idea. Even if the world later discovered that others had the idea first, or made working lightbulbs before him, it's natural that people would still remember and use the association with Edison. Whoever is most visible in bringing something new will forever be associated with that thing. Ask any four-year-old who invented pancakes, and odds are high she'll say, "My mom." If we've been exposed to only one source for something, how could we imagine others?

This tendency extends to the names of things. As a kid, I laughed when my grandparents called every refrigerator "Fridgidaire"— the first brand of consumer refrigerator in America (1919)[5]—until I realized I often use brand names, such as Kleenex, Band-Aid, Ziploc, Frisbee, or Post-it Notes, as many people do, in similarly incorrect fashion.[6] Since those were the names I first associated with their respective innovations (tissues, adhesive bandage strips, resealable bags, etc.), they stayed with me. Even though I now know some of them were not the first brand to exist, or when I'm aware I'm using a similar product made by a competitor, I often thoughtlessly use the wrong name.

Ford and Edison paid for marketing campaigns to promote their innovations, businesses, and themselves. As businessmen, they had every reason to promote their work in ways that suggested they deserved every last drop of credit. They became media darlings of their times, appearing in interviews and books, and benefiting— just as star CEOs of today—from the power of public attention. It became convenient for journalists to write in an Edison- or Ford-centric view because making the inventors star characters increased the public's interest in the news, helping to sell more newspapers.

---

5 http://www.fundinguniverse.com/company-histories/Frigidaire-Home-Products-
Company-History.html.

6 In 2006, Harris Interactive published a brand study of the product names that have the strongest dominance and recognition for that product line. Other dominant brand names are Heinz (ketchup), Clorox (bleach), and Hershey's (chocolate): http://www.harrisinteractive.com/news/allnewsbydate.asp?NewsID=1063.

Innovators became easy heroes in America; people preferred to believe, and tell, positive stories about them rather than the less interesting, and more complicated, truths. Would anyone in 1917, during WWI, have cared to know that the Duryea brothers, and not Ford, started the first American car company?[7] Or that Ford owed homage to Leonardo da Vinci, Karl Benz, and others with strange names from foreign lands? Those details, no matter how honest, painted a complex and less patriotic story, which writers on competitive deadlines avoided. The small oversights that were necessary to cram complex truths into simple hero-shaped tales were convenient and comfortable for everyone—from newspapers to journalists to readers and their heroes—and it still happens today.

One popular example is Apple, Inc., well recognized as the innovative company behind the user-friendly Macintosh, the iPod, and the iPhone. However, history shows that the first products of those types were made by others years earlier. The first graphical user interfaces, mice, and desktop computers were developed by Xerox PARC and SRI systems in the 1970s, nearly a decade before Apple's first Macintosh in 1984. The first iPod, sold in 2001, was late to the game by years—digital music players from SaeHan, Diamond Multimedia, and Creative Labs, using flash memory and similar core design concepts sold in the late 1990s. And of course the Sony Walkman, first sold in 1979, was the true progenitor of the idea of personal, portable music. Mobile phones have a similarly long history, dating back to Martin Cooper's prototype at Motorola in 1973 (Cooper, as the legend goes, made the first cell phone call to his rival Joel Engle at Bell Labs, informing Engle he'd lost the race[8]). Apple, like Edison, earned well-deserved credit for vastly improving existing ideas, refining them into excellent products, and developing them into businesses, but Apple did not invent the graphical user interface, the computer mouse, or the digital music player. Similarly, Google did not invent the search engine, and Nintendo did not invent the video game. They deserve credit for many things, but other companies established the ideas and proved the concepts behind them. We want innovation explained in neat packages, but we also want to acclaim the right

---

[7] http://www.loc.gov/rr/scitech/mysteries/auto.html.

[8] http://news.bbc.co.uk/2/hi/uk_news/2963619.stm.

people for the right reasons—rarely do both happen simultaneously, unlike the invention of things themselves.

The challenge of simultaneous invention

Have you ever arrived at a party or work to find that someone is wearing the same shirt, pants, or shoes as you? It's a curiosity of modern life that we convince ourselves our wardrobes are unique, despite selecting the items from department store racks filled with dozens of the same shirts, slacks, and blouses. An observant shopper watching the goings on at the mall can easily imagine someone—roughly her size—heading home with a similar outfit. Yet if she ever does meet her fashion doppelganger at a party or on the street, she is astonished: "How could *she* wear something from *my* wardrobe?" Once obtained, regardless of how or why, we take conceptual possession: "That shirt with those pants is my idea."

Fashion is a good metaphor for the problem of simultaneous inventorship: the situation when two or more people claim to have invented something. Like wardrobe collision, it seems improbable in the moment that two people could unintentionally invent the same thing around the same time; stepping back, it's easy to see why it happens. The invention of calculus, television, telephones, bicycles, motion pictures, MRI imaging, and automobiles all involve various kinds of simultaneous, overlapping, or disputed origins.

It's common because innovations demand prerequisite knowledge—inventing a new cocktail (e.g., The Berkun[9]) requires experience with different liquors, and creating a new dance step (e.g., The Edison) demands knowledge of choreography. This narrows the number of people who could create a particular innovation. Add the limited number of popular problems in any field, and suddenly the number of people chasing particular challenges isn't so large.

---

9 Nominations for recipes for the drink "The Berkun" can be submitted at *http:// www.scottberkun.com/contact*. Entries that include sarcastic ingredients such as "bad writer juice" or "idiot schnapps" will be disqualified. Winner receives paid vacation to Hawaii (total lie).

For example, there are only so many people today working on better word processors, photo-sharing websites, or email applications. They go to the same industry events, read the same books, and see the same progress among mutual competitors—not to mention the shared experiences that come from being alive at the same time (and at a good time). In *Creativity in Science,* Dean Simonton explains:

> Galileo became a great scientist only because he had the fortune of being born in Italy during the time when it became the center of scientific creativity. Similarly, Newton's creative genius could appear only because he lived in Great Britain when the center had shifted there from Italy. If Galileo and Newton had switched birth years without changing national origins, then neither would have secured a place in the annals of science.[10]

Given the combination of shared factors, odds are reasonable that people in the same field, at the same time, studied in the same universities or learned from the same textbooks.[11] They might even have mutual friends, drinking buddies, or dance partners, making the chances for simultaneous invention unexpectedly high: as free as people are to think creatively, there is a wardrobe of existing ideas that they're all shopping from.

What makes simultaneous invention (also known as *multiples*) contentious is that creators often work in isolation from—yet in competition with—their peers, making them prone to fantasies that their creations are unique. In the case of calculus (an innovation that destroyed my college GPA), two brilliant minds made the same conceptual leap, independently: Isaac Newton and Friedrich Leibniz separately developed systems for calculus. In that particular case, the inventions were offset by time, so they weren't technically simultaneous: Newton didn't formally publish his work until 1693; Leibniz published in 1684. Despite their love of reason, things were ugly in the scientific community as debates raged over which man was the rightful inventor—for years

---

10 Some believe in the zeitgeist theory of innovation—that cultural forces tell the true story of innovation. How else can we explain the Western Renaissance, Enlightenment, and Dark Ages without looking at the entire environment? From this viewpoint, individuals pay a large debt to factors beyond their control.

11 Malcolm Gladwell's book *Outliers: The Story of Success* (Little, Brown and Company, 2008) makes similar claims about often-overlooked factors in success stories.

England and Germany, Newton's and Leibniz's respective nations, used different versions of calculus, each one claiming righteousness out of national pride.[12]

More recently, the invention of television involved a five-way overlap of creative effort more complex than the Newton/Leibniz debate. Paul Nipkow was the first to consider sending images over wires back in 1884, but he never made a working prototype. In 1907, A. A. Campbell-Swinton and Boris Rosing were the first to suggest cathode ray tubes, but it wasn't until Vladimir Zworykin and Philo Farnsworth—working separately in the 1920s—that true working models of television existed. The inventors worked independently but simultaneously at the same basic goals with trails of overlapping concepts, progressions, and business politics too complex to follow. Like most innovations, if you crack open the invention of television in search of singular answers, you find more questions (which we'll explore later in this chapter).

One solution would be to clarify what it means to be "the inventor." As Brian Dickens, a software engineer explains:

> It is open for question whether "inventor" should suggest the person who came up with the initial idea for an item, the first person to build a working model, or the first person to successfully commercialize the invention. Obviously, for a new technology to ever make it into practical use, all three of these steps must be taken—but they will never be made all at once by the same individual, with no outside influences.[13]

It's smart advice. The problem is the sizable work involved in sorting out these details. The convenience of collapsing these facts down into a simple story is hard to resist.

The myth of the lone inventor

Everyone knows that Neil Armstrong was the first person on the moon. But how many people helped him get there? Of course

---

12 In *The Engines of Our Ingenuity*, John H. Lienhard writes, "That riddle dogs all of science. Equally futile arguments rage over who discovered oxygen. Was it Priestley who first isolated it? Lavoisier, who recognized it as a new substance but failed to identify what the substance was, or Scheele, who got it right before either Priestley or Lavoisier but didn't publish until after they had?"

13 *http://www.acmi.net.au/AIC/DICKENS.html*.

there was the rest of the crew: Buzz Aldrin and the oft-forgotten Michael Collins. Then, just like in the movies, there were the dozens of worried-looking mission-control staff on the ground, and notables like Wernher von Braun—intellectual forces who drove the entire program.[14] But what about the people who made the many complicated parts needed to construct *Apollo 11*? And what about the managers, designers, and planners who conceived the ideas, organized engineering teams, and coordinated years of work? The numbers add up fast. More than 500,000 people worked on the NASA effort to put a person on the moon. Armstrong's success required contributions from an entire metropolis worth of people, not including the millions of taxpayers who paid the bills, and the president who challenged a nation to believe. Neil Armstrong is a household name only because his contribution was the most visible. However, the most visible contribution isn't necessarily the most significant.

The fact that we know the names Neil Armstrong, Leonardo da Vinci, or Frank Lloyd Wright is an innovation all its own. If you want to know who designed the Egyptian pyramids, the Roman Coliseum, or the Great Wall of China, you're out of luck: no one knows. It wasn't until the 1500s and the rise of the Renaissance that Western cultures grew comfortable acknowledging people's creative abilities and individual achievements (we covered this briefly in Chapter 2). In *The Maze of Ingenuity*, Arnold Pacey writes, "Creation had previously been thought of as the prerogative of god; now it was seen as activity in which mankind could share...." While the inventors of the compass, the sword, or the mechanical clock missed their chance to make the history books, most inventions since the Renaissance have been credited to one or more individuals.[15] Until then it wasn't important or culturally acceptable to document who deserved credit for creativity.

This shift came with baggage: not everyone was allowed in the special "creative" club. The only people with creative license were

---

[14] *http://en.wikipedia.org/wiki/Wernher_von_Braun*.

[15] For example, the inventors of duct tape are unknown because the rise of corporations has clouded individual credit for many innovations. Johnson & Johnson produced duct tape for the military in 1942. However, duct tape is arguably a modified version of masking tape, invented decades earlier by 3M. If curious about its infinite uses, see *The Jumbo Duct Tape Book*, by Jim Berg and Tim Nyberg (Workman Publishing Company, 2000).

geniuses, the Michelangelos and da Vincis, whose talents seemed to stretch beyond human limitations. The rest of us, ordinary as we are, were expected to happily extend our worship to include these superhumans. Yet, these people, for all their brilliance, rarely worked alone. They shared their meals, romances, and daily lives with others, from ordinary shopkeepers to honest craftsmen, who influenced them and their work in many ways. Raphael, Plato, and Edison all had apprentices (in fact, when they were young, they worked as apprentices to older masters). They studied the great works of their time and had significant aid from unnamed assistants in making their masterpieces. They also benefited from powerful friendships: da Vinci was a pal of Machiavelli, and Michelangelo was childhood friends with Pope Clement (who, as an adult, would commission many great works from him).

Rivalries played roles, too: would Michelangelo or da Vinci, motivated by their mutual dislike for each other, have produced the same masterpieces if stranded on separate deserted islands? Michelangelo hated painting, and the Sistine Chapel was likely motivated in part to show up da Vinci. Would Coke be the company it is today without Pepsi? Microsoft without Apple? Take the supporting factors away, and the supposedly sole innovator doesn't seem superhuman anymore.

To be fair, those innovators are still amazing and awesome in their own right. Replacing Michelangelo with Britney Spears, or Edison with my dog Max—while leaving all other forces intact— would produce zero masterpieces (though Max is pretty smart). But the work of these individuals was far from solo or divine. If you look hard, you can find rare individuals who do achieve greatness in isolation—Tesla and Newton were notorious loners— but they are so rare, and their behavior so eccentric, that they are tough examples to learn from.

Today, years away from the Renaissance, we're still attached to the myth of lone inventors. We do recognize collaboration and partnerships, but we often fall back on tales of lone innovators as heroic figures for reasons of convenience. We insist on isolating credit and dismissing the importance of others. Patent law, by design, credits one or a handful of individuals, assuming not only that ideas are unique and separable, which is dubious, but that individual names can be given legal ownership of ideas. Patents, as currently applied in the U.S., do solve problems, but they create just as many. They distort popular understanding of how inventions happen, as well as which innovations are most valuable to the world.[16]

Guy Kawasaki, author of *Rules for Revolutionaries* and former Apple fellow, argues for demystifying lone invention. In his experience, great innovations and businesses are born when two or more creators work together to make things happen. He recommends:

> *Find a few soulmates. History loves the notion of the sole innovator: Thomas Edison (lightbulb), Steve Jobs (Macintosh), Henry Ford (Model T), Anita Roddick (The Body Shop), Richard Branson (Virgin Airlines). History is wrong. Successful companies are started, and made successful by at least two, and usually more, soulmates. After the fact one person may come to be recognized as "the innovator," but it always takes a team of good people to make any venture work.*[17]

Grand partnerships are easy to find: John Lennon and Paul McCartney, W. S. Gilbert and Arthur Sullivan, Bill Gates and Paul Allen, and Larry Page and Sergey Brin.

Stepping-stones: the origins of spreadsheets and E=mc²

When new TVs or mobile phones sit on store shelves, they seem self-contained. The experience is designed to inspire awe: innovations are featured on shrine-like displays with no signs of their manufacturing—all finished, polished, and gift-wrapped in plastic, waiting to be taken home. But if you look under the cover of any innovation, the magic of self-containment fades. There are subinventions, subproducts, minor breakthroughs, and parts and components, each with a story of its own. Every wondrous thing is composed of many other wondrous things.

---

[16] For example, one in five people in the world doesn't have clean drinking water, and one in four doesn't have reliable electricity. Few patents filed this year will be of use to them. See *http://news.bbc.co.uk/2/hi/science/nature/755497.stm*.

[17] Guy Kawasaki, *The Art of the Start: The Time-Tested, Battle-Hardened Guide for Anyone Starting Anything* (Portfolio, 2004), 10.

In *The Engines of Our Ingenuity*, John H. Lienhard writes:

> *The smallest component of any device, something so small as a screw, represents a long train of invention. Somebody conceived of a lever, someone else thought of a ramp, and another person dreamed up a circular staircase. The simple screw thread merges all of those ideas, and it followed all of them...each part represents a skein of invention, and the whole is a device that we would normally not see in the parts alone.*

Mobile phones and DVD players have dozens of screws—not to mention transistors, chips, batteries, and software. Take any of those pieces, divide again, and there's even more innovation hiding inside. It's easy to forget that the innovations we use are composed of a series of smaller innovations. However, making new things requires taking apart other things and learning from the pieces. Sometimes inventors even work the other way, developing breakthroughs by deliberately experimenting with existing innovations.

The first killer app, the software that legitimized personal computers, was the spreadsheet.[18] Before VisiCalc was released for the Apple II in 1978, most of the world did budgets, accounting, and business planning on paper.[19] VisiCalc was the reason computers shifted from geek toys to mainstream business problem-solving tools. Dan Bricklin, one of the creators of VisiCalc, developed the idea while pursuing an MBA at Harvard. In his mind, the birth of VisiCalc came from a combination of existing ideas (count the previous innovations he mentions in this short passage):

> *I would daydream. "Imagine if my calculator had a ball in its back, like a mouse..." (I had seen a mouse previously, I think in a demonstration at a conference by Doug Engelbart, and maybe the Alto) "...imagine if I had a heads-up display, like in a fighter plane, where I could see the virtual image hanging in the air in front of me. I could just move my mouse/keyboard calculator around, punch in a few numbers, circle them to get a sum, do some calculations, and answer '10% will be fine!'"[20]*

---

[18] Killer app, or killer application, is a name given to the first software on any computer that drives purchasing of the computer itself. See *http://en.wikipedia.org/wiki/Killer_application*.

[19] For entertainment and historical purposes, you can download a PC version of the original VisiCalc. It's useful if ever you forget how far we've come. See *http://www.danbricklin.com/history/vcexecutable.htm*.

[20] *http://www.bricklin.com/history/saiidea.htm*.

His early vision for VisiCalc involved calculators, mice, fighter planes, the paper spreadsheets he'd seen in his MBA classes, his frustrations with boring accounting assignments, and his awareness of what a computer programming language might be able to build. Naturally, as VisiCalc developed, the dependence on these ideas faded. Bricklin explains, "Eventually, my vision became more realistic, and the heads-up display gave way to a normal screen. The mouse was replaced in the first prototype in the early fall of 1978 by the game paddle of the Apple II." However, those ideas remained building blocks and inspirations. Remove one and VisiCalc may not have been made.

This theme of connections isn't limited to technology: you can find similar webs of innovation in all fields, from business to the arts to science. James Burke's famous book *Connections*[21] relentlessly explores the intertwined nature of inventions. Even the most famous five characters in the world, E=mc2, credited to Einstein, were based on concepts that came from many people. In David Bodanis' book, *E=mc2*, he explains how the work of Faraday, Lavoisier, Newton, and Galileo were the essential building blocks that made Einstein's formula possible.[22] Each contribution—*E* for energy, *m* for mass, and *c* for the speed of light—was a concept developed by others; Einstein's breakthrough was his approach in bringing them all together.

Despite the myths, innovations rarely involve someone working alone, and never in history has an invention been made without reusing ideas from the past. For all of our chronocentric glee, our newest ideas have historic roots: the term *network* is 500 years old, webs were around before the human race, and the algorithmic DNA is more elegant and powerful than any programming language. Wise innovators—driven by passion more than ego—initiate partnerships, collaborations, and humble studies of the past, raising their odds against the timeless challenges of innovation.

---

[21] James Burke, *Connections* (Little, Brown and Company, 1978).

[22] David Bodanis, *E=mc2: A Biography of the World's Most Famous Equation* (Berkeley Trade, 2001).

CHAPTER 6

Good ideas are hard to find

While I was waiting in a city park to interview someone for this book, a nearby child played with Silly Putty and Legos at the same time. In my notepad I listed how many ideas the young boy, not more than five years old, came up with in 10 minutes. Sitting in the grass, he combined, modified, enhanced, tore apart, chewed on, licked, and buried various creations I'd never have imagined. His young mother, chatting on a phone while resting her morning coffee on the park bench, barely noticed the inventive creations her kid unleashed on the world. After being chased away for making her nervous (an occupational risk for writers in parks), I wondered what happens to us—and what will happen to this boy—in adulthood. Why, as is popularly believed, do our creative abilities decline, making ideas harder to find? Why aren't our conference rooms and board meetings as vibrant as childhood playgrounds and sandboxes?

If you ask psychologists and creativity researchers, they'll tell you that it's a myth: humans, young and old, are built for creative thinking. We've yet to find special creativity brain cells that die when you hit 35, or hidden organs only the gifted are born with that pass ideas to their minds. Many experts even discount genius, claiming that the amazing works by Mozart or Picasso, for example, were created through ordinary means, exercising similar thinking processes to what we use to escape shopping mall parking lot mazes or improvise excuses when late for dinner.[1] Much like children, the people who earn the label *creative* are, as Howard Gardner explains in *Frames of Mind*,[2] "not bothered by inconsistencies, departures from convention, non-literalness...", and run with unusual ideas that most adults are too rigid, too arrogant, or too afraid to entertain.

The difference between creatives and others is more attitude and experience than nature. We survived hundreds of thousands of years not because of our sharp claws, teleportive talents, or regenerative limbs, but because our oversized brains adapt, adopt, and make use of what we have. If we weren't naturally creative and couldn't find ideas, humans would have died out long ago. A sufficiently

---

1   Robert W. Weisberg, *Creativity: Beyond the Myth of Genius* (W. H. Freeman, 1993).

2   Howard Gardner, *Frames of Mind: The Theory of Multiple Intelligences* (Basic Books, 1993).

motivated bear or lion can easily kill any man—even the meanest all-pro NFL linebacker. However, given creative problems to solve, an average human being is hard to beat. We make tools, split atoms, and have more patents than the world's species' combined (but please don't tell the bears—they get pissy about patents). Our unique advantage on this planet is the inventive capacity of our minds. We even make tools for thought, like writing, so that when we find good ideas—such as how to tame and cage lions—we can pass that knowledge to future generations, giving them a head start.

But with the advance of civilization, creativity may have moved, for many, to the sidelines. Idea reuse is so easy—in the form of products, machines, websites, and services—that people are enabled to go for years without finding ideas on their own. Modern businesses thrive on selling prepackaged meals, clothes, holidays, entertainments, and experiences, tempting people to buy convenience rather than make things themselves. I don't believe everyone should make everything themselves, or even most things. But I do believe everyone has the capacity to enjoy creating something, and the temptation for convenience inhibits many people from discovering what it is they'd like to make. Passive consumption of television and the Web has absorbed time we could be using for active hobbies and pastimes, age-old places for nurturing our creative selves. The need for craftsmen and artists, professional idea finders, has thus faded; more people than ever make livings in careers Lloyd Dobler would hate: selling, buying, and processing other things.[3] Even when charged to work with ideas, few adults can do so as easily as they could in their youth.

Einstein said, "Imagination is more important than knowledge," but you'd be hard-pressed to find schools or corporations that invest in people with those priorities. The systems of education and professional life, similar by design, push the idea-finding habits of fun and play to the corners of our minds, training us out

---

[3] Lloyd Dobler, played by John Cusack, is the main character in the film *Say Anything*. "I don't want to sell anything, buy anything, or process anything as a career. I don't want to sell anything bought or processed, or buy anything sold or processed, or process anything sold, bought, or processed, or repair anything sold, bought, or processed. You know, as a career, I don't want to do that." See *http://www.imdb.com/title/tt0098258/quotes*.

of our creativity.[4] We reward conformance of mind, not independent thought, in our systems—from school to college to the workplace to the home—yet we wonder why so few are willing to take creative risks. The truth is that we all have innate skills for solving problems and finding ideas: we've just lost our way.

The dangerous life of ideas

Quick test: Name five new ways to change the world, or you'll die!

Sorry, time's up. Fortunately, I can't kill anyone from this side of the book, and writers killing readers is bad business. But if I did honor the threat, you'd be dead. No one can come up with one big idea, much less five, that fast. As absurd as this paragraph is so far, it mirrors how adults often manage creative thinking: "be creative, and perfect, right now." Whenever ideas are needed because of a crisis or a change, there's a fire-drill call, an immediate demand. But rarely is the call met with sufficient resources— namely time—to mine those ideas. The bigger the challenge, the more time it will take to find ideas, but few remember this when criticizing ideas to death moments after they've been born.

Cynical idea-killing phrases like "that never works," "we don't do that here," or "we tried that already" are common (see "Negative things innovators hear" on page 57) and can easily make idea-finding environments more like slaughterhouses than gardens. It's as if an idea knocks on the door, and someone answers, waving his fist: "Go away! I'm looking for ideas." Ideas need nurturing and are grown, not manufactured, which suggests that idea shortages are self-inflicted. It doesn't take a genius to recognize that ideas will always be easier to find if they're not shot down on sight.

The myth that leads to this idea-destroying behavior is that good ideas will look the part when found. When Henry Ford made his first automobiles—awkward, smelly machines that stalled, broke down, and failed even the most generous comparisons to horses—people judged the superficial aspects, not the potential (see Figure 6-1). Everyone believes the future will come all at once in a neatly gift-wrapped package, as if Horse 2.0, whatever

---

4 See Neil Postman, *The End of Education: Redefining the Value of School* (Vintage, 1994), and Ken Robinson, *Out of Our Minds: Learning to Be Creative* (Capstone, 2001).

its incarnation, would make its first appearance with trumpets blaring and angels hovering above. The future never enters the present as a finished product, but that doesn't stop people from expecting it to arrive that way.

Figure 6-1. Would you see this idea—a flimsy gas-powered cart called the quadcycle—as the future of transportation in 1898? Most people then didn't either. This is one of Henry Ford's first automobiles.

The idea of the computer mouse (see Figure 6-2) was equivalently weird and uninspiring to pre-PC-age eyes ("Wow, a block of wood on a cord! The future is here!"). Evaluating new ideas flat out against the status quo is pointless. New ideas demand new perspectives, and it takes time to understand, much less judge, a point of view. Flip a world map or this book upside down, and at first it will feel bizarre. But wait. Observe for a few moments, and soon the new perspective will make sense, and might even be useful. However, that bizarre initial feeling tells you nothing about the value of the idea—it's an artifact of newness, not goodness or badness. This means using statements like "this hasn't been done before" or "that's too weird" alone to kill ideas is creative suicide: no new idea can pass that bar (see the sidebar "Idea killers" on page 90).

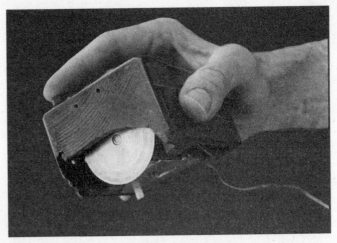

Figure 6-2. The superficials of innovation are rarely impressive. This is a version of the first computer mouse.

How to find good ideas

To open minds and find good ideas, return to the kid in the park. What is it about his attitude that allows fearless idea exploration? Linus Pauling, the only winner of two solo Nobel Prize awards in history, had this to say about finding ideas: "The best way to have a good idea is to have lots of ideas." This sounds idiotic to most ears because it cuts against the systematic, formulaic, efficiency-centric perspective worshiped in schools and professions. It seems wasteful to follow Pauling's advice. Can't we just skip to the good ideas? Optimize the process? Memorize a formula to plug stuff into? Well, you can't.

The dirty little secret—the fact often denied—is that unlike the mythical epiphany, real creation is sloppy. Discovery is messy; exploration is dangerous. No one knows what she's going to get when she's being creative. Filmmakers, painters, inventors, and entrepreneurs describe their work as a search: they explore the unknown hoping to find new things worth bringing to the world. And just like with other kinds of explorers, their search for ideas demands risk: much of what's found won't be satisfactory. Therefore, creative work cannot fit neatly into plans, budgets, and schedules. Magellan, Lewis and Clark, and Captain Kirk were all sent on missions into the unknown with clear understanding that they might not return with anything, or even return at all.

The lives of well-known creative thinkers were filled with compulsions for playing with ideas: they wanted wide landscapes to explore. Beethoven obsessively documented every idea he had, madly scribbling them on tree trunks or on the manuscript paper he had jammed into his clothing, even interrupting meals and conversations to scratch them down.[5] Ted Hoff, the inventor of the first microprocessor (Intel 4004) used to tell his team that ideas were a dime a dozen, encouraging them not to obsess or fixate on any particular one until a wide range of ideas had been explored. Hemingway made dozens of rewrites and drafts, changing plots, characters, and themes before he published his novels. WD-40 is named because of the 40 attempts it took to get it right (Dr. Ehrlich's cure for syphilis, called Salvarsan 606, was similarly named). Picasso used eight notebooks to explore the ideas for just one of his paintings (*Guernica*); if you watch the film *The Mystery of Picasso*, you can watch the master exploring ideas, good and bad, in real time as he creates dozens of paintings.[6] See Figure 6-3.

Figure 6-3. *Many artists use canvases to try out ideas as they paint—they're not painting by numbers, but exploring and making mistakes.*

5 Edmund Morris, *Beethoven: The Universal Composer* (HarperCollins, 2005).

6 The film *The Mystery of Picasso* (Dir. Henri-Georges Clouzot, Image Entertainment) is a classic of art schools everywhere. Few artists, much less legends, were as open to documenting their process as Picasso, as demonstrated by this film. Make sure to listen to the DVD commentaries, as they provide more insight than the sparse soundtrack. See *http://www.imdb.com/title/tt0049531/*.

Idea killers

These are phrases for thoughtless idea rejection. They're used by people who are too lazy to give useful criticism or direction, who fail to ask idea-provoking response questions, or who dismiss others not believed to have the potential for good ideas. Phrases like "it's not in our budget" or "we don't have time" are half-truths, as budgets and schedules can be changed for a sufficiently good idea. Others are idiotic, such as "we've never done that before," a condition of any new idea, good or bad.

- We tried that already.
- We've never done that before.
- We don't do it that way here.
- That never works.
- Not in our budget.
- Not an interesting problem.
- We don't have time.
- Executives will never go for it.
- It's out of scope.
- People won't like it.
- It won't make enough money.
- How stupid are you?
- You're smarter with your mouth shut.

A complete list of idea killers is at *http://www.scottberkun.com/blog/?p=492.*

In any field, creatives are those who dedicate themselves to generating, working, and playing with ideas. Pattie Maes, director of MIT Media Lab's Fluid Interfaces group, explains:

> *Most of the work that we do is like this. We start with a half-baked idea, which most people—especially critical people—would just shoot down right away or find uninteresting. But when we start working on it and start building, the ideas evolve. That's really the method that we use at the Media Lab...in the process of building something we often discover the interesting problems and the interesting things...that leads to interesting discoveries.*

There is further support for an innovator's desire to seek out new ideas. In a recent survey, innovative people—from inventors to scientists, writers to programmers—were asked what techniques they used. Over 70% believed they got their best ideas by exploring areas they were not experts in (see Figure 6-4).[7] The ideas found during these explorations often sparked new ways to think about the work in their own domain. And since they didn't have as many preconceptions as the people in that field, they could find new uses for what were seen as old ideas. Doctors studied film production; writers read biographies of painters. Any pool of ideas, no matter how foreign, could become a new area of discovery for an open mind.

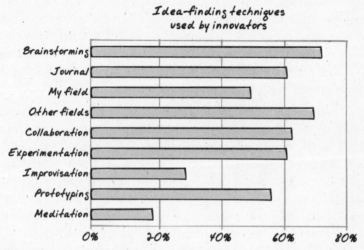

Figure 6-4. Based on a recent online survey of over 100 self-identified innovators in various fields.

As we saw with the child in the park, creativity is intertwined with the ability to see ideas as fluid, free things. Ideas come, they go, and that's OK; to an open mind, ideas are everywhere (something I'll prove shortly). It's the willingness to explore, experiment, and play, to invest energy, hit a dead end, and then chase a new direction that allows minds to find good ideas. All of our notions of play, and its freedoms from formal judgment, are inexplicably linked to finding good ideas.

---

7   *http://www.scottberkun.com/blog/?p=422.*

Ideas and filters

For all my trumpeting of open-minded thinking, it's true that wandering the Library of Congress looking at random ideas won't result in the Nobel Prize. We're asked to find ideas to solve problems, and even if idea finding approximates explorative play, it has to eventually wander back into something resembling work.

The secret to balancing work and play is thinking of the mind as a filter. Instead of binary switches—open vs. closed, creative vs. routine—we need a sliding scale of openness we can control. If you want new ideas, you have to slide toward openness, turning some filters off, exploring thoughts you'd ordinarily reject offhand. Do this until some interesting ideas are found; then, gradually turn more filters on until you're left with a handful that are both good and practical for the problem at hand. Choosing which filters to apply when has much to do with successful innovation; it's not just having an open mind, it's also knowing when to postpone certain judgments, and then when to bring them back in. If a mind is always open, it never finishes anything; if a mind is never open, it never starts.

Our brains and senses are designed, in part, to filter things out. Consider eyesight: at best we see 160 degrees around us, less than 50% of the visual information nearby. Dogs hear more sounds and cats smell more odors than we do. Even as children, we learn rules of conduct and behavior, both to be safe and to fit into society, filtering out possibilities. And, perhaps worse for creativity, as adults we aim for efficiency in our time, shortcutting through days, looking for fast tracks and power tools. The trap of efficiency is that it's not how explorers or inventors do their jobs: they turn their filters off for long stretches of time, trying to go where others haven't been. They wander into inconvenience, and danger, purposefully. Even when tasked with being creative, most people most of the time apply filters too soon.

The history and misuse of brainstorming

The term *brainstorm* has been abused and bastardized in the 50 years since its coinage. The concept originates with Alex F. Osborn, whose excellent book *Applied Imagination* launched the industry of business creativity books.[8] Its rise to popularity led to

---

8 Alex F. Osborn, *Applied Imagination* (Charles Scribner's Sons, 1957).

the quick misuse of the technique as a panacea for every conceivable business problem. When it failed to do the impossible of tripling people's IQs, reversing executive stupidity, or instantly transforming dysfunctional teams, the business world turned against it, despite its fundamental goodness. Those who still use the term apply it trivially to refer to any thinking activity they might need to do. The true essence of brainstorming as a method is well described in *Applied Imagination*, a fantastic read and a forgotten classic. The core message is simple:

- You have three things: facts, ideas, and solutions.
- You need to spend quality time with each individually.

The great mistake is leaping from facts to solutions, skipping over the play and exploration at the heart of finding new ideas. Most of us are experienced with finding facts—they're beaten into us throughout our education, and modern media pummels us with more. We're also familiar with solutions, which are the end results that pay the bills and explain why we've survived in the world. But idea finding? What's that? It's what few adults are patient enough to do, yet it's at the heart of creativity (the child in the park) and brainstorming (as defined by Osborn).

- **Fact finding.** The work of collecting data, information, and piles of research about whatever it is that needs to be done.
- **Idea finding.** The exploration of possibilities—free from as many constraints as possible—and using or ignoring facts as needed to find more ideas.
- **Solution finding.** The development of promising ideas into solutions that can be applied to the world.

Finding ideas and turning off filters

Osborn researched which environments stimulated people's creativity, and this study led to the following four idea-finding (aka brainstorming) rules:

1. Produce as many ideas as possible.
2. Produce ideas as wild as possible.
3. Build upon each other's ideas.
4. Avoid passing judgment.

Rule #1 sets the goal on volume, not quality (think Beethoven, Hoff, and Pauling). Since we don't know which ideas have value until we've explored them, spliced them together, or played with their many combinations, we need a big landscape. According to Osborn, a group of four or five properly led people can continually find new ideas for anything for a half-hour to an hour, producing 50 or 100 ideas before running out of steam (see his book *Applied Imagination*).

Rule #2 encourages crossing boundaries and saying illogical, unexpected, and unpredictable things. Since we naturally inhibit what we say for fear of embarrassment, if you set outrageousness as a goal and reward it, you help turn that filter off, opening up the chance to find interesting ideas. Sometimes asking for the worst ideas for a particular problem can take you in entertaining directions, leading to places you'd never otherwise go. Have you ever been lost in a bad neighborhood in a new city, only to find a fantastic shop or restaurant? Discovery can have any origin, and Rule #2 forces exploration. If nothing controversial, weird, or embarrassing is said in a brainstorming session, you've violated Rule #2.

Rule #3, like Dan Bricklin's combination of innovations to invent VisiCalc, encourages the combination of ideas to force creative thinking through hybrids and idea breeding. All ideas are made from other ideas. Making this explicit prevents people from suppressing ideas for fear of stepping on, or changing, an idea mentioned by someone else. NIH (Not Invented Here) syndrome, where ideas from others are rejected, is a clear violation of Rule #3.[9]

Finally, Rule #4 takes us back to the secret of the kid in the park. Judgment isn't necessary during exploration; we don't know enough about the possibilities, so why would we reject or accept any idea? Would you buy the first car you sat in? Marry the first sexy person you met? When finding ideas, everyone needs to know his ideas won't be judged until later. And if the goal is volume (Rule #1), there's no need to evaluate the initial thought, only to write it down so it can be explored later. Judgment is all too easy, and there's no harm in holding it back a while to give those ideas a fighting chance.

---

[9] A good review of NIH syndrome and approaches to avoiding it at the organizational level can be found in *Open Business Models*, by Henry Chesbrough (Harvard Business Press, 2006).

However, there are limitations. When done in groups, the human dynamics of social situations come into play. Is everyone trying to kiss up to the boss? Does Fred always hog the floor? Is Jack afraid to say anything? Designating a skilled facilitator keeps things flowing and fair, and ensures that the rules are followed and that the meeting runs only as long as needed. The vibe should approximate the playful environment of a park: a fun, low-stress, free time to try things out, awaken dormant imaginations, and take pleasure in chasing new ideas.

Proof that ideas are everywhere

One game, famous in improvisation, is called "What Is This?" Look at any object around you: a pen, a cup, this book. Ask yourself, "What else can it be used for?" Take, for starters, this book in your hand: it's a doorstop, a weapon, a plate, a way to get your boss to be less of an idiot, a waste of $20, and on it goes. Play this game with a friend and see who can come up with more ideas.

The point is that anything can be used for things other than its intended purpose. We assume everything has one function, but that's wrong: you can use anything for anything (although it might not work well, you can try). There's nothing stopping you from using this book as underwear or to paper your walls. The game forces you to turn your filters off.

Many great ideas come from the repurposing of one thing for something else. Laser beams were used to make CD players and supermarket checkout scanners. Even attempting to reuse something in a novel way, and failing, can lead to ideas no one else has thought of before. Play the game with items you use in your work or with failed projects just asking for reuse, and you'll soon find yourself off and running with an abundance of good ideas.

CHAPTER 7

Your boss knows more about innovation than you

What advice would typical executives give Stephen Hawking, one of the brightest living minds, if he worked for them? Would they ask him to write daily status reports? Defend his action items from PowerPoint slides at team debrief meetings? Of similar curiosity is whether Steve Wozniak, Albert Einstein, or Isaac Newton ever filled out time cards, wrote performance reviews, or had their ideas ranked on scorecards by committees of middle managers. Could you imagine Mozart, da Vinci, or Marie Curie sitting next to each other, taking notes, at an all-day company-wide event? It's hard to see any of these commonplace situations working out well for the prospect of innovation.

If we struggle to imagine past innovators doing amazing things in our workplaces, what makes us think we can do creative work in them? Talent is only as good as the environment it's in. If we threw Shakespeare or Bach into a creative dungeon, lashing them when ideas entered their minds, odds are against them being creative for long, if at all.

Few managers recognize that their training and experience, designed to protect what exists, work against the forces needed for innovation. The history of management—lurking beneath the hot trends of *Harvard Business Review* and *Fast Company* magazines—is rooted in factories, banks, and railroads, not in invention, creative thinking, or revolution. And while it's easy to see the impossibility of managing creative teams with the techniques of assembly lines, many managers do use these techniques, trapping good ideas in systems structured to work against them.

The myth that managers know what to do

Here's an experiment: close this book, look at the back cover, and turn it upside down. Really, do it. Please? Pretty please with sugar on top? Look, I'm the author of this book and I'm giving you a direct order. Do it now or I'll stop writing. I'll wait. (Imagine me at my desk, twiddling my writerly thumbs, bored out of my mind, waiting for you to stop reading this sentence and be an obedient reader, flipping the book to examine the back cover. Look, it's worth it, I swear on this book.) OK, now that you're back, let's chat about what just happened, in the context of power and talent.

Even if reading this book has been the worst slog of your life, I bet you checked the back cover anyway. The reason is simple: as the author, I have power. You assume I know what I'm doing. But there is a difference between power and talent. You didn't look at the back cover because of how talented I am: you did it because I, being the all-powerful god-like voice of the page, told you to. (Now, send me six frosted cupcakes, a case of pale ale, and 12 million dollars in small, unmarked bills.[1])

Similar confusion reigns in the workplace. Those in power can make decisions others can't, but that doesn't mean they have the wisdom or experience to do it well. Every rock-star innovator has worked for someone who couldn't innovate his way out of his pants. But we deny this because we often want to believe, despite evidence to the contrary, that those with authority are as talented as they are powerful. Faith in this idea makes working for them tolerable, as it offers an explanation (however false), for why *we* are working for *them*. There are exceptional managers out there, stars worthy of their power and more, but they're hard to find. The rest of the time innovators must beware of their own myth-making: it's easy to overlook peoples' lack of talent by misplacing faith in their power.

Why managers fail

This book has emphasized the point that no one knows what's possible. Every great innovation had dozens of leading minds laughing it out the door. Chester Carlson, the inventor of the first copy machine, was told the technology he needed would never exist. Lord Kelvin, one of the great physicists of the 19th century, said machines heavier than air could never fly. Right now, powerful managers, even the cute ones who appear on magazine covers, are failing to predict the future. There is no innovation oracle. Futurists, like Buckminster Fuller or Nicholas Negroponte (founder of MIT's Media Lab), make their livings being wrong most of the time.[2] It's beyond human comprehension to know with any certainty what will happen next.

---

[1] The psychology of authority is not a joke. The seminal Milgram experiments proved just how willing we are to torture each other simply because we are told to do so. See *http://www.holah.co.uk/summary/milgram/*.

[2] Buckminster Fuller coined the word *synergy*, among many others. It's a nice reminder that all words were invented by someone, and it's silly to bemoan the addition of new words to language.

Yet somehow when people bring a new idea to their manager, they forget the fallibility of prediction. It's easy to assume that the manager has a better perspective on the viability of an idea, perhaps from her superior experience and knowledge of the industry. But these are exactly the factors that also work against innovation: high experience and confidence make people the greatest resisters to new ideas as they have the most to lose (see "The innovator's dilemma explained" on page 61). The managers of propeller aircraft design were the last to adopt jet engines. Same for graphic user interfaces vs. command lines, telephones vs. telegraphs, and—as hard as it is to admit—for whatever we're using now vs. whatever is coming next.

It's natural for people to protect what they know instead of leaping into the unknown, and managers are no exception. Managers might even be worse, as the politics they rely on to survive can make them more entrenched and defensive. Peter Drucker writes, "Management tends to believe that anything that has lasted for a fair amount of time must be normal and go on forever. Anything that contradicts what we have come to consider a law of nature is then rejected as unsound." And since few managers are aware of these natural biases, or trained to overcome them, they're unprepared for the day the future—in the guise of a half-baked, curiously shaped idea—knocks on their door. It's not a question of intelligence or intention, it's a willingness to re-evaluate management's purpose.

The conflicts of management and innovators

Professional management was born from the desire to optimize and control, not to lead waves of change. Frederick Taylor, Henry Ford, and Henry Laurence Gantt (of charting fame)—the fathers of professional management—believed it should be a reductive science. The goal was to minimize chance, optimize performance, and take control away from individuals. Decades before the first MBA graduates dreamed of well-paying consulting jobs, Mr. Taylor studied the inefficiencies in factory workers; stopwatch in hand, he took notes, did time studies, and prescribed methods for faster performance. That's right: the making of widgets, hinges, nuts, and bolts is what drove the creation of business management.[3]

---

[3] You can find other management theorists before Taylor. The military has the oldest management traditions because they were the first with the need to organize large groups of people for controlled tasks.

Called scientific or classical management, the philosophy centers on designing jobs with repetitive tasks, and rewards the manager for optimizing the company's performance in measurable terms—for example, widgets made per minute (see Figure 7-1).

Figure 7-1. The management philosophy for running assembly lines can never create an innovation like the assembly line. Ford's first moving car assembly line, 1913.

If this seems like ancient history, remember that the automobile, oil, and railroad industries of the 19th and early 20th centuries fueled the economic growth of the United States. The success of these industries both legitimized Taylor and created wealth used to start or fund many well-known business schools of today (Vanderbilt, Stanford, Harvard, MIT Sloan, and others).[4] Despite how progressive some modern management programs are, their roots are in a tradition most unkind to innovation. Management as a discipline is steeped in an old-school command and control attitude that is alive and well in the Internet Age.

---

[4] Vanderbilt and Stanford, founders of eponymous universities, were railroad tycoons. Harvard Business School's first campus was funded by George Fisher Baker, president of the First National Bank. The MIT Sloan business school is named after Alfred P. Sloan, Jr., chairman of the board of General Motors.

To be fair, most management, most of the time, is sensibly directed at maintaining good business. It's hard enough to keep a business profitable and a team of people working together effectively; if an organization is healthy and successful, it makes sense for its leaders to act in ways that conserve those good things (although Taylorism isn't the way).[5] However, when managers raise the flag of innovation, the goals change, and the methods must follow. Many depend solely on Taylor-inspired behavior as a rule, regardless of what the goals demand. These folks are easy to spot: they might know buzzwords or talk of seeking breakthroughs, but they avoid all risks, never yield creative authority, and operate with self-centric hierarchical control over the flow of ideas. Like in an assembly line, these managers hold tight to the notion that they are the sole possessors of intelligence, and, as a result, must exercise regular control over workers capable only of the menial tasks of production.

Amy C. Edmonson, professor of management at Harvard Business School, agrees: "Management 101 is...based on the assumption that we know with a high degree of certainty what needs to happen...that is simply an outmoded concept, but we still use the same management tools: a production mindset...."[6] To lead innovation requires rethinking who a manager is, what success feels like, and which tactics work. And to do that, we have to look back at managers of past innovations.

Five challenges of managing innovation

I've reviewed the histories of hundreds of innovative projects from different industries, team sizes, and eras, and distilled five traits that managers of those efforts applied. Of course, this is not a guarantee: exceptions can be found of leaders following these and

---

5   Taylor was right about one thing: at the time, production was inefficient, and he deserved praise for asking new questions. However, he failed to empower workers by involving them in improving efficiency. Many workers have ideas for improvements and will suggest them if rewarded—a strategy Taylor never considered and which may have been more efficient than his own (were all those studies necessary? I can imagine workers laughing behind Taylor's back as he took weeks to discover inefficiencies they noticed their first day).

6   Kelley Holland, "Under New Management," *The New York Times* (November 5, 2006), *http://www.nytimes.com/2006/11/05/business/yourmoney/05mgmt.html*.

failing, as well as those who ignored them but still had success (see Chapter 3). However, the patterns are strong enough to apply widely, including to start-up companies, solo efforts, ad hoc groups, or even innovative projects in large organizations. No matter how many people are involved, these five challenges are faced by someone and must be overcome to bring the innovation to the world:

1. Life of ideas
2. Environment
3. Protection
4. Execution
5. Persuasion

The life of ideas

Ideas are everywhere. Chapter 6 explored some of the basics of creative thinking, but the life of ideas is bigger than what happens in brainstorming meetings. The best idea-finding sessions in the world are useless if that creative energy doesn't go anywhere. Ideas don't do much—it's what's done with them that matters. Are they funded? Encouraged? Used to reinvent and rethink? Given time to grow? Rewarded with cash prizes or trips to Hawaii? Are people pushed to explore, prototype, follow their instincts, and learn from what happens?

Teams with healthy idea life cycles are easy to spot: ideas flow between people easily and in large volumes. Conversations are vibrant with questions and suggestions; prototypes and demos happen regularly; and people commit to finding and fighting for good ideas. Often, this is fun—people are happy to learn from failures, debates, and bizarre ideas. Teams that innovate are great places for ideas to live; like happy pets, they're treated well, get lots of attention, and are shared among people who care deeply about them.

The life of ideas is the responsibility of whoever is in charge. He defines it by his responses and behavior, especially when he's challenged by someone else's ideas. For example, if someone asks, "Hey boss, can we have status meetings over lunch to save time?"

and the boss replies, "Say something that stupid again and you're fired," no one will ask similar questions. All ideas about improving the status meeting, and perhaps improving anything, are dead forevermore. Or, more typically, if no ideas from anyone other than the manager are ever chosen, people will eventually stop proposing suggestions.

Teams with scorched fields where creative jungles should be usually have a manager to blame. The boss must attend to the life of ideas for all the people he works with, investing time and money to nurture their young ideas, granting room for them to breathe, and supporting the ideas' development, delivery, and recycling (to make way for new ones).

The environment

Alan Kay, a member of the legendary group at Xerox PARC, said this about his manager, Bob Taylor: "His attitude kept it safe for others to put aside fears and ego and concentrate objectively on the problem at hand."[7] According to many accounts, Bob Taylor encouraged a free discourse of ideas, including open criticism and debate, in a weekly meeting in a room filled with beanbag chairs. The goal wasn't to roast each other, but to push, prod, cajole, share, inspire, and enrage as needed to give life to everyone's best ideas.[8] The environment put innovation at the center, with politics, posturing, and hierarchy on the perimeter. This can go as far as office architecture because people's ability to feel creative and share ideas is heavily influenced by how their offices, shared spaces, and buildings are designed.

Tom Kelley, general manager of IDEO and author of *The Art of Innovation*,[9] explains:

---

7 Douglas K. Smith and Robert C. Alexander, *Fumbling the Future: How Xerox Invented, Then Ignored, the First Personal Computer* (iUniverse, 1999), 79.

8 An excellent exploration of the manager's role in creative environments can be found in Jerry Hirshberg, *The Creative Priority: Driving Innovation in the Real World* (HarperBusiness, 1998). The book is based on his experience as director of Nissan design and explains the role of tension in creative environments (he calls it *creative abrasion*).

9 Tom Kelley et al., *The Art of Innovation* (Currency/Doubleday, 2001).

Innovation flourishes in greenhouses. What do I mean by a greenhouse? A place where the elements are just right to foster the growth of good ideas. Where there's heat, light, moisture, and plenty of nurturing. The greenhouse we're talking about, of course, is the workplace, the way spaces take shape in offices and teams work together.

Lewis Thomas, author of *Lives of a Cell*[10] and former dean of the Yale Medical School, writes:

One way to tell when something important is going on is by laughter. It seems to me that whenever I have been around a laboratory at a time when something very interesting has happened, it has at first seemed to be quite funny. There's laughter connected with the surprise—it does look funny. And whenever you hear laughter...you can tell that things are going well and that something probably worth looking at has begun to happen in the lab.

That laughter, in part, means people are comfortable with new ideas. The Nerf toys, open architecture, and fun vibe at Google's headquarters (see Chapter 1) aren't gimmicks; the environment is supportive of ideas and collaboration, which helps innovations move through the organization.

Hiring and team structure may define the working environment more than other factors combined. Bob Taylor hired with innovation in mind, recruiting people who naturally challenged the status quo and were self-driven pursuers of their imaginations. He wanted people who thrived on the uncertainties of doing new things, who could drive ideas forward. Taylor viewed his management role not as a grand creator or assembly-line foreman, but as an enabler of other people's ideas. And it worked—his team developed the laser printer, Ethernet, object-oriented computing, and the graphical user interface (GUI). Good managers of innovation recognize that they are in primary control over the environment, and it's up to them to create a place for talented people to do their best work.

---

[10] Lewis Thomas, *Lives of a Cell: Notes of a Biology Watcher* (Penguin, 1978).

The protection

One thing a genius can't do that her manager can is provide cover fire. Whether through power, inspiration, or charisma, managers have the singular burden of protecting their teams. Innovations always threaten someone in power, and executives in search of budget cuts frequently target them first. The manager's unique role is to use whatever means necessary to shield innovation while it's too young to defend itself in the open. Steve Jobs took the Macintosh project into a separate building at Apple headquarters, sequestering it from the rest of the company. The first laptop at Toshiba was rejected by corporate leaders, and Tetsuya Mizoguchi, the team leader, fought to keep the project alive until he won executive support. Three years later, the product had 38% of the market.[11] Any story of breakthrough work has someone acting as a shield, defending innovation while it's happening.

One of Thomas Edison's secret weapons was his star persona. His ego may have been large, but he used his stardom as a shield for his research lab: his true engine of innovation. His team of bright minds—a dozen inventors in Menlo Park, New Jersey—worked happily in relative anonymity, free from public scrutiny or the stresses of appearances and interviews. Many major insights of developing the electric light and the phonograph are attributed to his staff, not to Edison himself. Edison took the heat for ideas that failed, and by making himself an easy target for investors and the public, he protected his team from all kinds of negative influences.[12]

All innovations run on political capital: the lifeline of budget and staff comes from somewhere, and everyone (including the project leader) is in competition for those limited resources. Even famed start-up companies that began in garages had to be defended from frustrated spouses or sarcastic teenagers who wanted those resources for more traditional purposes (families are as political as any organization). Life is a zero-sum game, and the resources for innovation must come at the expense of something else.

Successful innovators compare their ambitions to their capital. If a project needs more time, money, or political cover fire than its

---

11 From *Diffusion of Innovations*, 145.

12 Andrew Hargadon, *How Breakthroughs Happen: The Surprising Truth About How Companies Innovate* (Harvard Business School Press, 2003).

leader can provide, the effort will be exposed prematurely, lobotomized, or killed. For example, if the manager bets on promises for budget (or loans) that are withdrawn, or makes claims that he fails to deliver, the effort will die of starvation no matter how many great ideas, creative environments, or amazing talents it has. And if he's too conservative and doesn't take enough risks, the project might survive, but it will not be progressive enough to achieve its goals. It's a tightrope to walk—pushing a project hard enough without pushing it too far—but every successful innovator has done the same balancing act since the beginning of time.

Protecting innovation includes obtaining funds, finding allies, protecting teams from natural predators (defenders of status quo, jealous managers, the ever-resilient and contagious threat of organizational idiocy), and even buffering the team and its stars from their self-destructive tendencies. Sometimes protecting an innovative team will demand withholding information that might discourage the team (for example, a VP's napalm-laced feedback), testing the manager's judgment, boundaries, and willingness to make psychological sacrifices for the project. Managers can take larger bullets for the team than anyone else.

The execution

Ideas are abstractions. You can't get cash from the idea of an ATM, nor commute home on the notion of a hovercraft. To become an innovation, an idea has to blossom into whatever form necessary—a demo, a prototype, a product—to be useful to people. To shepherd an idea down the long, arduous path from conception to realization is known as *execution*. And despite its workman-like reputation in comparison to creative thought, executing on an idea is the hardest task faced by managers of innovation. In Chapter 6, we explored how easy ideas are to find; the challenge is doing all the work necessary to manifest them in the world. We know the names Edison, Wright, Wozniak, and Tesla not because they had grand ideas alone, but because they were able to execute on them before their competitors. Steve Jobs was right when he said, "Real artists ship," to rally the Macintosh team into putting in the long, exhausting, unglamorous hours needed to get the product out the door.[13]

---

[13] *http://www.folklore.org/StoryView.py?project=Macintosh&story=Real_Artists_ Ship.txt.*

Execution forces managers to deal with the countless details that were waved away during brainstorms and demos. All the challenges swept under the rug of "we'll deal with it later" or "that's not important now" become immovable roadblocks, demanding immediate attention, otherwise progress stops. These sacrifices are often difficult for idealists to handle. Even though their passion is what convinced others to support their ideas, that passion must be tempered by compromises if those ideas are to make it to the world.

The challenge is making the right sacrifices at the right time in the right way: there is no formula for this, only the manager's and her team's judgment. Managers must balance the team on the edge of the ideals that drove the effort through early stages ("We will change the world!") and the necessary constraints of schedules and budgets to finish ("We must ship in four weeks, do or die"). Too much idealism, and the work never ships—not enough, and little change is brought to the world.

Persuasion

Innovation champions—like Jeff Hawkins (Palm), Steve Jobs (Apple), and Bob Taylor (Xerox PARC)—have often needed to put down their swords and egos to pitch their projects for all they're worth. Innovators never have all the cards, so they must ask others for help to make things happen: start-ups have investors, films have production companies, and businesses take loans from banks. Earlier, we explored why people don't like new ideas, as well as the questions people with new ideas face. Well, this is true for managers, but the stakes are even higher: they're not only responsible for their ideas, but also for the collective hopes of an entire team.

All innovation heroes survived the closing of doors in their faces: Carlson (Xerox), Jobs (Apple II), Page and Brin (Google), and Smith (FedEx). As persuasive as these greats might have been, they weren't convincing enough to prevent rejections. We imagine great persuaders as charismatic figures, dazzling and romancing the soon-to-be-convinced with special powers, but real innovators are not magicians. The difference between success and failure is most often relentlessness, not talent or charisma (though those help).

Jobs explains, "I'm convinced that about half of what separates the successful entrepreneurs from the non-successful ones is pure perseverance."[14] Persuasion is a skill; if sufficiently motivated, anyone can improve.[15]

Persuasion is needed to start a project, recruit top people, obtain resources, convince talent (or a spouse) not to leave, as well as to compel investors or customers to buy once there is something to sell. Persuasion fuels innovation at all levels, and every successful innovation depends on getting people to believe in things that have not been done before.

---

[14] *http://americanhistory.si.edu/collections/comphist/sj1.html.*

[15] Robert B. Cialdini, *Influence: Science and Practice* (Allyn & Bacon, 2000).

CHAPTER 8

The best ideas win

The best ideas don't always win, but that doesn't stop people from believing they should. Most innovators were frustrated by how their ideas, clearly superior in their own minds, struggled for acceptance in the world. Pick from any field at any time and you'll discover tales of dismay, depression, and anger fueled by the innovators' faith that their better ideas not only should, but would win out over others. Of course, visionary innovators are rarely objective in these matters, as often these so-called best ideas are conveniently their own.[1] Ted Nelson, the man who coined the phrase *hypertext*, laments the limitations of the World Wide Web, and he continues to fight for big ideas that predate the web browsers by decades. Douglas Engelbart and Alan Kay, pioneers of the personal computer, have similar exasperations about the grand ideas they pioneered in the 1970s that have yet to be realized.[2] Even social and political innovators like Martin Luther King, Gandhi, and Thomas Jefferson voiced similar righteousness about their ideas and the faith that the best ones should prevail.

It's not news that innovators are often idealists, but the myth that the best ideas win should not be underestimated. Notice how few people run around arguing that the worst idea wins or that their own inventions are rubbish. People have beliefs about what the world is or should be, and why some ideas, inventions, or people win out over others. Even the notions of best, good, win, and lose are opinions, as is the obsession with framing things in binary terms. Good vs. bad, best vs. worst, happy vs. sad are all tenuous constructions, as the world never divides into two easy piles (e.g., happy vs. sad neglects the existence of the bittersweet). However, that doesn't stop people from trying.

---

1   I've yet to find a solid reference for the relationship among egos, innovation, and achievement. One general reference is *Greatness: Who Makes History and Why*, by Dean Keith Simonton (The Guilford Press, 1994). However, as an anecdote, the wide majority of biographies I've read about great innovators include great egos.

2   Doug Engelbart has done many interviews about his perception on his place in history, as well as the state of computing today. One example that briefly mentions his opinion of the current state of computing can be found in this short essay: *http://queue.acm.org/detail.cfm?id=1039523*. Alan Kay has also offered many commentaries on the state of technology relative to better ideas being ignored; some of these ideas are touched on in this interview: *http://www.educause.edu/ir/library/html/erm/erm99/erm99027.html*.

It's clear at this point in the book that innovation is complex, has many meanings and factors, and can't be captured in the pithy quotes that make for good myths. As this chapter explains, there are many perspectives, and it's impossible to remember them all, all the time. This is why the myth that the best idea wins is so dangerous. It plays possum, rolling on its back, looking cute and innocent, while it quietly reaches behind our backs, taps on our far shoulders with its furry little paw, and laughs as we turn away from the truth.

Why people believe the best wins

Fairy tales and hero stories follow similar patterns: good guys win, bad guys lose, and people who do the right thing get nice prizes.[3] These rules are pleasant, easy to remember, and have been with us as long as we've had stories to tell. In some cultures, including America, these stories of "goodness wins" extend to intellectual goodness and the making of good things. Americans hold ingenuity to be one of the best kinds of goodness, spotlighting it and projecting it into our local history: Benjamin Franklin's political inventiveness; the innovative tactics of minutemen in the Revolutionary War (which weren't that innovative); and the industrial genius of Whitney, Fulton, Edison, Ford, Carnegie, and Steve Jobs. By the simplest definition, heroes are the best at what they do. America created Superman, not *Second-place*-man or *Sometimes-better-than-average*-man.

Meritocracy—the ideal that the best do or should win—is a deeply held belief among Americans, and in part comprises the American Dream. Combined with the hero model (good guys win), there's a natural tendency to nudge the telling of history toward stories that fit both ideals and to whitewash, or ignore, those that don't. Whenever we don't know the full story of why someone or something won, the default assumptions are:

1. The victory was deserved: "Edison made the first lightbulb."

---

[3] Of course, mythologies and fairy tales are numerous, and there are many patterns equally as prominent in various pantheons as wish fulfillment and hero quests. See *The Uses of Enchantment*, by Bruno Bettelheim (Penguin, 1991), or *The Hero with a Thousand Faces*, by Joseph Campbell (Princeton University Press, 1972).

2. The victory was heroic: "Gutenberg paved the way for the Internet."

Certainly most know that the best doesn't always win, but we don't go out of our way to uncover counterexamples either (much like the discussion in the section "Evolution and innovation" on page 25). We accept stories that fit the patterns we know, as they provide happy feelings and encourage hope for how life *should be*. Victors of the past who won with dubious ethics or for questionable reasons—like Rockefeller, Carnegie, or even Achilles—are remembered not for their flaws or unpopularity in their own time, but as heroes of achievement. Their victories and benevolent contributions, truths that fit the mythology, are the most popular stories we tell about their lives.[4] And should bad decisions have been made, given enough time, the reasons for those judgments often fade, leaving only traditions of respect. Consider that the Liberty Bell, which cracked in half when first struck in 1753 and again decades later—clearly not well made or heroic in any way—is now a worshiped artifact of American history.[5] Or that Alfred Nobel, best known for founding the Nobel Peace Prize, made his fortune by inventing dynamite.[6]

The pantheon of fictional legends popular in America includes MacGyver, James Bond, Indiana Jones, John McClane (from the film *Die Hard*), and Captain Kirk, invincible heroes who defeat evil at overwhelming odds by using good ideas, guile, and a healthy serving of gratuitous violence. They have better ideas, so they win. We're fond of creative idealism even at extremes, such as in stories like Ayn Rand's *The Fountainhead*, in which Howard Roark, a heroic architect, places his ideas above everything.

---

4 The *robber barons* are easy targets. Despite the label, today they're recognized primarily for their philanthropic works, universities, and foundations. Carnegie had several incidents regarding workers' rights, including the Homestead Strike of 1892 in which Frick, a manager under Carnegie, led the lockout of employees, resulting in a riot and a dozen deaths. The icing on the ironic cake is that the park next to Carnegie Mellon University in Pittsburgh is named Frick Park, and most students know his name for this reason alone. See *http://www.pbs.org/wgbh/amex/carnegie/peopleevents/pande04.html.*

5 The Liberty Bell didn't get its name until 1835. It has quite a story of misfortunes, some of which are likely myths themselves. See *http://www.libertybellmuseum.com/resources/faqs.htm.*

6 Nobel was enigmatic, so not much is certain about his view of his own work. However, the creation of the Nobel Prizes happened at his death as specified in his will.

Despite the complexity of the tale, the protagonist willingly sacrifices for his ideas. The simpler message often taken from this epic novel is that good should win over bad, and if a better idea is ignored, the world is to blame ("the hostility of second-hand souls"). This belief goes further than meritocracy—the world's sense of what is best is less important than the individual's.

Applied to business, the myth that goodness wins is best captured in the famous saying "If you build a better mousetrap, the world will beat a path to your door." It's sometimes paraphrased as "If you build it, they will come," the iconic quote from the baseball film *Field of Dreams*. Unfortunately, the phrase is misattributed to Ralph Waldo Emerson, a leading 19th-century intellectual. What he actually said was probably, "If a man has good corn, or wood, or boards, or pigs to sell, you will find a broad, hard-beaten road to his house."[7] I'm not sure when you last sold pigs or grew corn, but Emerson had something other in mind than rallying would-be entrepreneurs to get in the innovation game. The phrase was meant to be poetic, not instructional, and he'd be disappointed at how many people have taken his words literally.

The phrase has been used as the entrepreneur's motto, misguiding millions into entertaining the notion that a sufficiently good idea will sell itself. As nice as it would be for good ideas to take responsibility for themselves, perhaps using their goodness ID cards to cut ahead of stupid ideas in the popularity line, it's not going to happen. Even the (false) proverbial mousetrap, as historian John H. Lienhard notes, has about 400 patents for new designs filed annually in the U.S., and we can be certain that no one is beating down their doors.[8] More than 4,000 mousetrap patents exist, yet only around 20 ever became profitable products. These days, the best equivalent to the metaphoric mousetrap is "to build a better website," proven by the 30,000 software patents and 1 million websites created annually.[9] Certainly not all of these efforts are motivated by wealth or wishful thinking, but

[7] Jack Hope, "A Better Mousetrap," *American Heritage*, October 1996, vol. 47, issue 6 (online at *http://www.americanheritage.com/articles/magazine/ah/1996/6/1996_6_90.shtml*).

[8] Ibid.

[9] *http://www.realgeek.com/230/us-software-patents-hit-record-high/*.

many inventors still hope that the "If you build it, they will come" sentiment is alive and strong.

Lienhard, based on his study of innovations throughout history, challenges that faith:

> Rarely if ever are the networks that surround an innovation in its earliest stages given the credit they are due...a better mousetrap, like anything else, will succeed only when those who envision the idea convince others to join in their new venture—as investors, suppliers, employees, retailers, customers, and even competitors.

The goodness or newness of an idea is only part of the system that determines which ideas win or lose. When we bemoan our favorite restaurant going out of business ("But they make the best cannelloni!") or why our favorite band can't sell albums ("They have the best lyrics!"), we're focusing on a small part of the picture that affects us personally, which is only one factor in the circumstances determining its fate. These environmental, or secondary, factors have as much influence as the quality of the idea, talent, or innovation itself.

The secondary factors of innovation

The history of innovation reveals many ideas that dominate a field yet are derided by insiders. Any high-tech device today follows the QWERTY keyboard model, a system designed for neither efficiency nor ergonomics. The Phillips screw is inferior to the lesser-known Robertson screw, a clever gem of industrial design.[10] The M-16, one of the most widely produced rifles in the world, initially had serious jamming and ease-of-use problems.[11] Fireplaces, staples in American cabins and homes, are one of the least efficient heating systems known to man. And HTML and JavaScript are far from the best software development languages, yet they're

---

[10] Witold Rybczynski, *One Good Turn: A Natural History of the Screwdriver and the Screw* (Scribner, 2001). See *http://inventors.about.com/od/sstartinventions/a/screwdriver.htm.*

[11] This is a disputed claim, and its accuracy depends on time. During the Vietnam War these complaints were frequent, but some claims since the 1970s point to improved ammunition and other modifications that nullify these problems. I'm not an expert on this issue, but I did find enough evidence to confidently list it in this paragraph. Start with *http://www.time.com/time/magazine/article/0,9171,843858,00.html.*

perhaps the most successful in history. The list goes on, despite the best wishes of all the smart, goodness-motivated people throughout time. Even today, right now, ideas of all kinds that experts criticize—including those in your own fields of expertise—are gaining adoption.

In Chapter 4 we explored the psychology of innovations' diffusion, listing how individuals make choices that impact innovation adoption. Now, it's time for a broader analysis of influential factors. Looking at history, here are seven factors that play major roles:

- **Culture**. Firearms were most likely invented in China in the 1200s, but for a variety of cultural and geographic reasons, they didn't develop as quickly there as they did in Europe centuries later.[12] Some Asian cultures viewed swords and old styles of fighting as more honorable, and despite the military advantages of using firearms, they were ignored (a sentiment echoed by the Jedi in *Star Wars* films). The best technology is only one view of innovation—how the innovation fits in a culture's values is often stronger. For example, imagine a device in the U.S. that gave you telepathy at work but required you to make lunch out of your neighbor's dog or be naked in public, two taboos of American culture. Innovations do change societies, but they must first gain acceptance by aligning with existing values.

- **Dominant design**. The QWERTY keyboard came along for the ride with the first typewriter. When Christopher Sholes created this layout, he didn't imagine millions of people using it—he just needed a design that wouldn't jam his mechanical keys. But once typewriters succeeded, the first computer designers wanted to ease people's transitions to their creations, so they copied the typewriter design. Many dominant designs achieve popularity on the back of another innovation. Better designs might follow, but to gain acceptance, they must improve on that dominant idea by a sufficient margin to justify the costs of the switch (e.g., relearning how to type). The more dominant the design, the more expensive those costs are

---

[12] Kenneth Chase, *Firearms: A Global History to 1700* (Cambridge University Press, 2003).

(e.g., try innovating, or unifying, the shape of electric plugs around the world).

- **Inheritance and tradition.** The U.S. rejection of the metric system is tied to tradition: America already knew the English system, so why learn another? (See "Space, metrics, and Thomas Jefferson" on page 119.) Some people confuse their comfort for a belief with it actually being good. As a result, inherited ideas (including the evils of bigotry, ignorance, and urban legends) are often protected by the very people they hurt in order to honor the beliefs of their parents and the past. This is a specific cultural factor.

- **Politics: who benefits?** There's often little malice in political workings—people are simply acting in self-interest. In any situation, just ask: who benefits if we choose X, and who benefits if we choose Y? You can predict how people in power will respond to any new idea if you first calculate its impact on them. The interests of those in power influenced the adoption, or rejection, of every innovation in history. Hunger, war, and poverty are tough problems, but if someone is profiting from these problems, there will be powerful forces encouraging them to continue. Any innovation aimed at solving those problems must consider politics in order for it to succeed.[13]

- **Economics.** Innovation is expensive: will the costs of changing to the new thing be worth it? Everyone might agree that an innovation is better in the abstract, but the financing required might be impossible or the risks unreasonable. Dominant designs (see above) are expensive to replace. Often there is only time or money for innovating in one area—other innovations are rejected, not on their merits, but on their value to the priorities of the moment.

- **Goodness is subjective.** Get three people in a room and you'll get five definitions of goodness (see Chapter 10). Fireplaces, mentioned earlier, are popular because of how they look more so than how they function. Consumer differences in values, tastes, and opinions are rarely explored until after an innovation has been proposed, or even built, leaving innovators with

---

13 "If you want to understand a new technology, ask yourself how it would be used in the hands of the criminal, the policeman, and the politician." —William Gibson

creations the public does not want. Smart innovators study their customers, mastering their needs early enough that those factors can be useful. The often-used Beta vs. VHS example fits: a key factor in the success of VHS was tape length (three hours, enough for a feature film, to Beta's one hour), which was more important to consumers than Beta's superior video quality.[14]

- **Short-term vs. long-term thinking.** One part of goodness is time: how long does this innovation need to be used for? Many superior ideas are rejected by societies interested in cheaper, shorter-term gains. In the 1930s, major cities in the U.S. had public transportation—trolleys and tram systems modeled on successful designs from Europe. But in the rush of the 1950s, and the thrill of automotive power, those street-cars were removed and replaced with new lanes for cars. Today, many cities regret these changes and approximate trol-leys with new light-rail systems. The goodness of ideas changes depending on how far into the future their impact is considered.

The next time you witness a great idea rejected, or a bad idea accepted, this list will help reveal the true factors at work. Up next is an examination of two innovations, revealing how these sec-ondary factors have played out in the past.

Space, metrics, and Thomas Jefferson

On September 23, 1999, NASA's $300 million Mars *Orbiter*, flying through space millions of miles from Earth, fired its engines to slow into orbit around Mars. Its 10-month journey complete, the craft flew silently above the Martian sky at a leisurely 12,000 miles per hour. It followed all its programmed instructions and was, as planned, turning behind Mars' dark side, disappearing for the first time. The command staff waited expectantly for the *Orbiter* (see Figure 8-1), 10 years in the making, to reappear on the other side. Ten minutes later, well past its expected timeline, it had not arrived. Mission control feared the worst. They searched the Mars atmosphere but there was nothing: the *Orbiter* was gone.

---

[14] *http://www.guardian.co.uk/technology/2003/jan/25/comment.comment.*

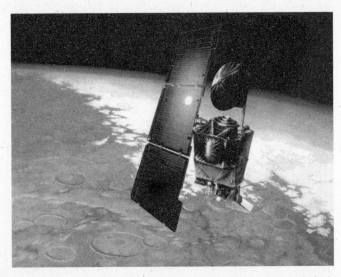

Figure 8-1. The poor little Mars Orbiter. Had Jefferson succeeded, the craft might have survived its trip to Mars.

They'd learn later that the spacecraft entered the wrong orbit, flying too low. Instead of a routine trip around the planet, it approached at a deadly angle and was destroyed in the atmosphere. What took longer to understand was the cause. Somehow, somewhere, an equation failed to convert units from metric to English, and the $300 million *Orbiter* was sent on a path of certain destruction. It was doomed before it even launched.

As is always the case, this failure had many causes. The *Orbiter* was part of the "Faster, Better, Cheaper" initiative at NASA to accelerate innovation by removing processes in the name of creative freedom. But it simultaneously increased risks—a common dilemma for managers of innovation (speed cuts both ways). One link in the chain of failures is the metric system itself: why does the world, and particularly the U.S., still use two different systems of measurement?

The metric system has been in use for over 200 years. It's used by 190 of the 193 nations on this planet, and it has many advantages over the English system (explained shortly).[15] Cans of soda, like

---

[15] As you'd expect, there is no end to the debate over the relative merits of English and metrics, as well as the costs of switching in the U.S. For details on international use of the metric system, see *http://lamar.colostate.edu/~hillger/*. For pro and con arguments, check out these sites: *http://www.metric4us.com/* and *http://ts.nist.gov/WeightsAndMeasures/Metric/mpo_home.cfm*.

Coke or Pepsi, still list both English and metric measurements (12 oz/354 ml) as an odd testament to a token compromise of policy—and a good idea ignored. Even the United Kingdom, the home of the English (foot/gallon/mile) system, moved on to metrics decades ago.

The American story of metrics, a tale of proposed and denied innovation, begins with Thomas Jefferson. While serving as Secretary of State, he innocently proposed to the U.S. Government that they replace the English measurement system.[16] It's an odd mess of ad hoc measurements from the Babylonian, Roman, and Saxon royalty, and it wasn't a system so much as a pile of half-baked traditions and blindly followed rules (see "Inheritance and tradition" on page 118). The yard, for example, was defined by the length of the belts worn by kings (had they not been so rotund for their day, who knows what size our football fields would be). Endorsed by English monarchs through the ages, the system was adopted without question by the American colonies. But Jefferson was smart and a free thinker. He knew it wouldn't be hard to design a better system, and that it would be a great value to the new nation. He got to work and soon had a plan similar to what would be called metrics by France years later.

He divided the English foot into 10 units called lines, and divided lines into 10 units called points. Using tens, decimal math, made perfect sense to him as an easy way to convert between unit sizes. (Quick: how many ounces in a gallon? Cups in a quart? We have 10 fingers, so base-10 math makes many operations easy.) He made a similar decimalization of larger measures—adjusted the size of the foot, yard, and mile to fit scales of 10—and proposed this plan to Congress in 1789. Everything was great. He probably imagined decimalizing everything from units of time to expressions of love. The promise in young Jefferson's mind must have been high.

The proposal landed with a thud (approximately 4.5 kilograms of force per cubic centimeter). Congress didn't so much reject his plan as starve it to death: the idea was ignored (in the previous list, see "Politics: who benefits?", "Economics," and "Short-term vs.

---

[16] Here's Jefferson simple proposal: *http://avalon.law.yale.edu/18th_century/jeffplan.asp*.

long-term thinking"), and time went on. Across the Atlantic, the metric system was ratified in France in the 1790s and spread over the decades into Europe's dominant system (although it was a slow, rocky process).[17] The opportunity for metrics to become dominant had much to do with the French Revolution, which ended just before metrics were ratified. As a general lesson, large innovations, say, political revolution, bring with them many smaller changes for better or for worse. The metric system rode the wave of political innovation in France in a similar way to how the QWERTY keyboard rode the wave of technological innovation of the typewriter.

In 1866, the rise of the metric system forced the U.S to respond despite passing on the same idea 75 years earlier. Congress took action, but it was far from decisive. They drafted an act stating it was now legal—not required or encouraged, but legal—for people to use the metric system if they chose.[18] With an endorsement like that, how could the metric system lose? That's like parents telling their children they're now allowed to clean their rooms thrice a day. Few Americans were moved, and the English measurements remained. There was little motivation for individual business owners to convert their equipment, no matter how much better Jefferson—or anyone objective on the subject of measurement—thought the system. Several more anemic attempts were made to promote metrics, including the requirement for foods to be dual-labeled with metric and English measures (thus the soda cans), but to this day, no further effort has been made.

Some think situations like metrics in America need a forced hand: the only way a leap can be made is by mandate. For fun, imagine that you had evidence that replacing the QWERTY keyboard with a different design would create world peace or guarantee survival of the human race. What would have to be done to replace it around the world? In a single large country? In less than six months? Tasks like these are difficult because the costs of change are astronomical. Unless, like QWERTY's adoption, there is a larger wave of innovation that takes a replacement for QWERTY

---

17 http://www.sciencemadesimple.com/metric_system.html#History.

18 http://lamar.colostate.edu/~hillger/laws/metric-act.html.

with it (or as is popular in sci-fi films, does away with keyboards entirely), it would be hard to make any progress at all.

Some innovations—such as safety systems in automobiles or environmentally safe home construction (e.g., asbestos-free)—succeeded only because governments provided incentives or penalties as motivation (in some cases, making the dominant design illegal). How else can progress happen in situations where the collective benefit for a society is greater than the perceived benefit for individuals? (For example, mandated elementary school is good for society, but unpopular with children). However, some believe that forcing the hand of innovation goes against the nature of free markets and often backfires. The truth is complex: sometimes forcing innovation adoption works, and sometimes it doesn't. The best lesson in all cases is that success is defined more by the factors listed previously than by who is pushing the innovation—and how hard they're pushing it. Having $50 million to market a product means little compared to the forces of culture, dominant design, and politics.

To fully apply those factors to this example, the English system was the dominant design. While metrics had advantages, no one convinced the American politicians or people why the costs of making the changes were worth the effort. Thinking politically, what interests would be served by a businessman or a politician making the switch? And after Jefferson left office, why wasn't anyone willing to lead the charge for his proposal? The minority of those who benefited were set free after the Metric Act of 1866, but anyone on the fence never received incentive for change.

The goodness/adoption paradox

> *The best is the enemy of the good.*
> —Voltaire

Another excellent example of the tenuous relationship between an idea's goodness and its success is the technology behind the World Wide Web. When Tim Berners-Lee invented the Web, he didn't have the future of technological development in mind. His tool of choice for making websites, called HTML, reflected simple notions for what documents would be like in the future. He didn't imagine the Web would have its own economy with bookstores and banks, nor was he thinking about the billions of personal and professional websites that would become our primary way to interact with information. Instead, he thought about scientific research papers, text-heavy one-way communication, because that's what the organization he worked for worried about.

His passion for simplicity was so great that he initially downplayed the role of images and media, focusing instead on text. For his purposes, HTML was lightweight, simple, and easy to learn. Why weigh it down with the unnecessary features of other programming languages? He explicitly wanted something easier than the complex tools used for making software programs so that people could easily make web pages. In 1991, the first web server was up and running, and Berners-Lee's colleagues soon made their own websites and web pages.[19]

In 1993, there were 130 websites, but within six months, that number more than quadrupled. By 1995, there were over 23,000; the number would continue to double annually.[20] The simplest word processor was all anyone needed to participate, so participate they did—much to Tim Berners-Lee's and the entire world's surprise.

At the time, many computer science experts lamented how slow, un-secure, and immature the technology was behind the World Wide Web. And many still do today. They believe they know better, and that if they could go back in time and tell Berners-Lee or the folks at Netscape—makers of the first commercial web browser—what to do, all those problems would be solved (there certainly would never have been a blink tag).[21] The fallacy is that if they had their wish, they'd end up with an entirely different, and possibly not so successful, World Wide Web. Although the Web is struggling to retrofit privacy, security, and other good things, had they been in place in 1993, they may have raised barriers to entry, slowing or preventing the growth of the Internet we know today.

The factors that spread innovations, from the personal ones listed in Chapter 4 to the broader ones listed earlier, are largely about

---

19 *http://www.w3.org/People/Berners-Lee/ShortHistory.html* and *http://www.w3.org/History/1989/proposal.html.*

20 *http://www.mit.edu/people/mkgray/growth/.*

21 Even the inventor of the blink tag regrets it: *http://en.wikipedia.org/wiki/Blink_element.*

ease of adoption. The reason why Internet and cell phone usage climbed faster than previous technologies isn't because things happen faster today. (Nor is it because these technologies are bigger leaps forward than previous ones.) It's simply because the barriers of entry were low. People already had PCs and phone lines, making Internet use cheap and easy (economics). For cellular phones, the population already had daily experience with personal telephone usage and cordless phones, and their frequent use was accepted social behavior (culture). If you think about it, the cell phone isn't more than a cordless phone with unlimited (well, sometimes) range. The Internet and World Wide Web, for all their wonders, were an extension of the PCs and modems already in use—AOL had trained millions to use email, and word processors were popular applications on those computers.

The goodness/adoption paradox surfaces if, for fun, we separate goodness (from the expert's point of view) from the factors that drive adoption (see Figure 8-2). From the expert view of goodness, better technologies existed for publishing and networking than Berners-Lee's Web. Ted Nelson and Doug Engelbart had talked about and demoed them for decades. But those "better" ideas were demanding in ways that would have raised barriers to adoption in 1991. At best, they would have cost more to build and taken more time to engineer. We can't know whether those additional barriers would have prevented the Web from succeeding or merely have changed its ascension. It's also possible these alternative web designs might have had advantages that Berners-Lee's Web didn't have, which would have positively impacted ease of adoption.

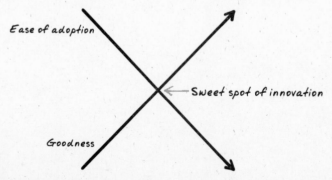

Figure 8-2. The notion of goodness described by experts often competes with ease of adoption.

This suggests that the most successful innovations are not the most valuable or the best ideas, but the ones that appear on the sweet spot between what's good from the expert's perspective, and what can be easily adopted, given the uncertainties of all the secondary factors combined. The idealism of goodness and the notion that goodness wins is tempered by the limits and irrationalities of people's willingness to try new things, the culture of the era, and the events of the time. This explains why the first innovators—driven by complete faith in their ideas—are so often beaten in the market, and in public perception, by latecomers willing to compromise.

CHAPTER 9

Problems and solutions

Living alone in a wooden townhouse miles from London, Isaac Newton worked endless hours alone by candlelight. Stacks of papers, journals, and notes from experiments littered the small manor that was his home. Beyond explaining gravity, inventing calculus, and revolutionizing science, his true passion—which fueled his pre–Electric Age all-nighters—was turning lead into gold.[1] This 18th-century search for the philosopher's stone—a method for changing one element into another—occupied many great minds including Bacon, Boyle, Locke, and Leibniz, and was believed to be the greatest technological challenge of the age. One can only guess at how many collective months these most brilliant minds wasted chasing the impossible. For all his genius, Newton may as well have been banging his head against the wall (perhaps preparing him for getting hit by apples), as the laws of physics we know today render his work a waste of time (see Figure 9-1).[2]

Figure 9-1. *This painting of Newton, by William Blake, shows him as a lost hero. Blake felt that Newton's attempts to solve everything through science and alchemy were misguided.*

---

1   *http://www.pbs.org/wgbh/nova/newton/alch-newman.html.*

2   However, simply because the laws of physics today suggest Newton was wrong doesn't mean he was. A breakthrough in our understanding of energy, matter, or particle physics could reveal Newton was right about the possibility of the philosopher's stone.

Some say all innovation is a leap of faith, but the sensible (or at least those with mortgage payments) wonder about this: can you know when you're chasing the equivalent of a holy grail, a philosopher's stone, or a perpetual motion machine? Before entrepreneurs and inventors bet their lives on an idea, they want to know that it's achievable. And if it is, do they possess the talents and passions required to make it happen? If Newton, one of the great minds of history, can wander for years down an innovator's dead end, how can a merely bright mind expect to filter the possible from the impossible? The only hope for answers is to look past this mythology: problem solving is not nearly as important as problem finding.

Newton's mistake was the problem he chose, not his methods for solving it. Problem finding—problem solving's shy, freckled, but confident cousin—is the craft of defining challenges so they're easier to solve. Newton's choice set him up to fail before he began, and many bright would-be innovators make similar mistakes: they fail to spend enough time exploring and understanding problems before trying to solve them.

Problems as invitations

The word *problem* often means something bad, as in "Houston, we have a problem" or "I have a problem with your tuna salad," but successful innovation often involves more attention to problems than solutions. Einstein once said, "If I had 20 days to solve a problem, I would take 19 days to define it," a gem of insight lost in the glory of what he achieved on that 20th day. It's counterintuitive because, on the surface, problems rarely need help to be understood. For example, if Bob's pants are covered in flaming napalm, and Jane is being chased by rabid zombie Rottweilers, do they really need to sit and ponder before taking action? In everyday experience, a problem is something we want to get rid of quickly; for example, we know that Bob should rip off his pants, throw them at the Rottweilers, and whisk Jane away, with pants-free charm, for a heroically romantic afternoon.

But the challenges innovators choose have no known solutions or aren't believed to be important at all. No one asked Galileo to explain the solar system, Engelbart to invent the mouse, or Bell to create the telephone. They saw unidentified problems in the world and dedicated themselves to defining and solving them. Einstein's motivation for developing his special theory of relativity, while working as an unknown patent clerk, wasn't that his girlfriend thought it'd be cute. Nor did his boss threaten to fire him if he didn't win the Nobel Prize. Being curious of mind, he followed his own logic and asked questions others were unwilling to ask, and when he saw no answers, he simply set about finding his own.

Discovering problems actually requires just as much creativity as discovering solutions. There are many ways to look at any problem, and realizing a problem is often the first step toward a creative solution. To paraphrase John Dewey, a properly defined problem is partially solved.[3] And if your particular innovation involves the support of other people, a clearly defined problem helps form bonds and build teams where none existed before. Author John Seely Brown once said, "When we get in the spirit of following a problem to the root, that pursuit of listening to the problem brings multiple disciplines and multiple crafts together. The problem pulls people together."[4]

Framing problems to help solve them

One way to creatively describe a challenge is to compare it to another kind of challenge that's been solved. Scott Cook, the founder of Intuit (makers of Quicken and QuickBooks software), felt that the problem to solve wasn't making good accounting software, but something else entirely: "The greatest competitor...was not in the industry. It was the pencil. The pencil is a tough and resilient substitute. Yet the entire industry had overlooked it."[5] He creatively framed the problem and shifted the perspective of his team to find a better solution than pencil and paper. Even if his competition had more talented problem solvers, engineers, or designers, his creative framing of the problem gave him an advantage. Anyone can use Cook's basic framing strategy; by choosing a

---

3 That is: "A well-stated problem is half-solved." John Dewey was an American philosopher and education reformer in the early 20th century. Though inventor Charles F. Kettering may have actually said this quote.

4 From an interview in *Breakthrough: Stories and Strategies of Radical Innovation*, by Mark Stefik and Barbara Stefik (MIT Press, 2006).

5 From *Harvard Business Review on Innovation* (Harvard Business School Press, 2001).

powerful reference (the pencil), and framing the challenge around it (sell software), he created opportunities before he wrote a line of code.

This pattern is everywhere in the history of innovation, but it's often hidden behind tales of brilliance and breakthrough solutions. As a test, follow the trail of any successful innovation far back enough, and odds are high that you'll find a creatively framed problem behind it. While Edison is heralded for the lightbulb, he was late to the party: dozens of other inventors were trying well before he began. His success came from defining the challenge differently. He thought of the lightbulb as a system, asking questions like "How do you get power to homes to power the lightbulb? And where does that power come from?" A lightbulb alone was useless, and Edison knew why.

Cities had invested millions in gaslights, making any switch to a new technology incredibly expensive—even if there were perfect, cheap lightbulbs for sale. Ever the businessman, Edison was unwilling to make great lightbulbs that no one could buy. The real task to him wasn't to make a working lightbulb, as we're commonly taught. Instead, Edison framed the problem, and aimed to make an electricity system cities could use to adopt his lights. It's no surprise his philosophy of invention was based on 1% inspiration and 99% perspiration.[6] With so much confidence in the problems he chose to undertake, he knew it was only a matter of time before he succeeded. Edison avoided challenges like the philosopher's stone, or today's (lack of a) grand unified theory of physics, knowing that not enough pieces were in place yet for success to be possible.

A similar story of well-framed problems comes from the rise of personal digital assistants (PDAs). For decades, people talked about handheld devices that could manage your calendar, contacts, and personal information. The 1980s and early 1990s saw HP, Siemens, Sharp, and Apple invest millions in new products,

---

[6] Tesla, a rival of Edison's—who many believe was a superior inventor—had this to say about Edison's approach to inventing, "If Edison had a needle to find in a haystack, he would proceed at once with the diligence of a bee to examine straw after straw until he found [it]. I was a sorry witness of such doings...a little theory would have saved him ninety percent of his labor." From *The Engines of Our Ingenuity*.

which all failed. It seemed that a successful PDA might be like Newton's philosopher's stone—an impossible task. That was until the Palm Pilot, introduced in 1996, successfully overcame the challenges that stumped their competitors; PDAs became a billion-dollar industry, influencing the design of computers and mobile phones forever.

The key factor in Palm's success was that they defined their challenge differently than their competitors. Instead of focusing on engineering constraints, or lofty dreams of revolutionizing computers, they focused on what customers wanted. Jeff Hawkins, the founder of Palm, reasoned that his team knew as much about consumer feedback on previous PDAs as their competitors. Why not start the conversation with what people clearly needed, rather than what the companies of the day could provide?

Hawkins spent an evening at home with a notepad, and soon had the following list of goals for the Pilot project:[7]

- Fit in a shirt pocket
- Sync seamlessly with PC
- Fast and easy to use
- Not more than $299

In 1994, all of these goals were beyond ambitious—they were impossible. If you had shown them to any of the PDA companies of the day, you'd have been told to go home. But Hawkins realized solving these problems was the only real path to success. Handwriting recognition, color displays, or fancy keyboards were all nice ideas, but they weren't essential. If Palm could succeed at meeting these four challenges, Hawkins was convinced it had high odds of success.

Look carefully at those four bulleted items: there is great power packed into every one. Notice that the goal wasn't to be small, or handy, but specifically small enough to fit in a shirt pocket. It's an insightful criterion because shirt pockets are a time-tested size for various objects (lighters, cigarette packs, business cards, and most relevant to Palm, calculators), and by framing the challenges in this way, they focused their problem-solving efforts in ways that

---

7 Andrea Butter and David Pogue, *Piloting Palm: The Inside Story of Palm, Hand-spring, and the Birth of the Billion-Dollar Handheld Industry* (Wiley, 2002), 73.

would pay off. When Hawkins made the list, he didn't know how he'd satisfy those conditions, but the act of spending time framing them was time well spent. But sadly, despite its initial years of great success with the Palm Pilot, competitor HP eventually purchased a struggling Palm, Inc., in May 2010 for a mere $1.2 billion.

Other famously innovative projects were based on similar definitions. The book *Blockbusters*, by Gary S. Lynn,[8] examines many of them and how they came about (see Table 9-1). What's most interesting is how simple these objectives seem; because of their clear identification of the problem to solve, they're more powerful than complex ones. It's hard to forget these simple descriptions, so they make for useful tests of ideas as they're being developed.

Table 9-1. Famous projects and their goals (from Lynn, except Backpack).

PROJECT	PROBLEM DEFINITIONS/GOALS
Apple IIe	Reduce costs Simplify manufacturing Modernize Look like the Apple II
Original IBM PC	Beat Apple Do it in one year
Palm Pilot	Fits in shirt pocket Sync with PC Fast and easy to use Not more than $299
37signals Backpack[1]	Life's loose ends Basecamp is overkill Pages with simple tools Remind me away from the computer

[1] Backpack is an innovative web-based organizing tool. Backpack's list was used by permission from its creators at *http://www.37signals.com*.

The Palm Pilot's success came largely from its simplicity as a product—a quality driven entirely by the self-defined constraints. In *Piloting Palm*, by Andrea Butter and David Pogue, a book on the history of the Pilot's development, these criteria enabled decision makers to keep the product so easy to use.

[8] Gary S. Lynn, *Blockbusters* (Collins, 2003).

Hawkins, who presided over these meetings, was unyielding when it came to keeping what he saw as nonessential features out of the product. If the new machine were to fail it wouldn't be because it had been junked up with unnecessary functions, like its predecessors.... Soon the team became experts at killing features.[9]

The team's ability to focus on the core constraints—elements necessary for successful innovation—is what made the greatness of the Pilot possible.

Framing the problem by picking strong goals is nothing new: consider the Ten Commandments, the U.S. Bill of Rights, or even the rules for good games. Michael Jordan would never have dunked if James Nesmith had set the height of basketball hoops at 25 feet instead of 10. Hank Aaron wouldn't have hit 755 home runs if the inventors of baseball had decided that a ball hit over the fence was, perhaps most logically, out of bounds. Just like the creative talent of your smartest designer, programmer, or business analyst, picking the right problems to solve and defining them carefully creates a playing field for their talents. It's deceptively hard to create good constraints, and there's less glory in problem finding than solving; however, the number of successful innovations based on clever constraints proves it's worth the time.

Exploring problems with prototypes

If tomorrow at work you found the smartest person in your company sitting at his desk, typing away at a computer, monitor, and mouse all made from wood—without any electronics or working parts of any kind—what would you think? As for the Pilot's development, the true story is that Hawkins designed a wooden model. Early on, after framing the challenge with tough goals, he went to the small shop in his garage and spent hours sawing and carving. Although this wasn't easy, some decisions were straightforward because of the constraints: there were only a handful of ways to design a device to match the criteria. For example, to fit in a shirt pocket, the device could only carry AAA batteries—no other power source could work in that form factor. So, his model assumed AAA. Similar thinking forced decisions about screen size,

---

[9] From *Piloting Palm*, 81.

leading to the choice to go without a keyboard (and Hawkins whittled down a chopstick for use as a makeshift stylus). In a matter of hours, he had a prototype for the Pilot that he brought to work with him the next day.

He carried it around with him to all his meetings, pretending to use it as if it were the finished product. He'd "write" on it, carefully taking it out of his pocket and putting it away, to the dismay of the engineers and marketers on his team. They must have wondered why, for a cutting-edge technology project, their leader would carry around a roughly carved, nonelectronic replica of something that hadn't even been designed yet.

The value to Hawkins was obvious: how else could he explore? He wasn't certain that the problem of "design to fit in a shirt pocket" was the right form factor. It was possible that its shape should be like a banana or perhaps a Rubik's Cube. Or maybe there was another criterion, one they hadn't even imagined, that could only be discovered by using the model. To Hawkins, there was no other way. In his words, "An essential part of innovation is to envision the new product or service. You have to use it and experience it before it is designed and built." When dealing with complex problems and many unknowns, innovation happens only when smart ways are found to test designs against the challenges.

Anyone who has studied any creative field—painting, engineering, music, writing, and even filmmaking—knows there's nothing new here. Picasso spent hours with preliminary sketches before painting his masterpiece *Les Demoiselles* (he said, "To model an object is to possess it"). The Wright brothers built the first wind tunnel in America just so they could learn more about the airplane prototypes they made. In innovation, there is no alternative; the problems are too large to be attacked in any conventional way.

The truth about serendipity

When Dr. Percy Spencer found a melted candy bar in his shirt pocket while playing with some radar equipment, he had every reason to throw it away. Odds are good that other people in radar laboratories around the world experienced similar globs of chocolate and other foodstuffs in their pockets and did nothing about them, other than to clean up the mess and get back to work.

And given that the rational, logical parts of most intelligent people's brains would tell them to do the same (getting rid of the offending sweet bits and forgetting about it as soon as possible), it's entirely odd that Spencer chose to do something different. Remember, he essentially found a bit of warm trash in his pocket and decided to spend the rest of the day playing with melted cocoa beans, ignoring the millions of dollars of supercool top-secret defense equipment surrounding him in the lab.

Imagine Spencer in that magical moment: alone in the lab, expensive lights blinking all around, his eyes staring down at two chocolaty fingers, his Hershey-stained clothes and lab coat desperate to be washed. If you walked past him at that instant, you'd think for certain he was insane: a chocolate-fingered loon. But although he didn't know it yet, this chance encounter—the moment that red-lined his curiosity well past his logical mind's ability to follow—would lead him to the invention of the microwave oven. Curious about the source of heat, he put some popcorn kernels, and then an egg, by the nearest radar tube. The popcorn popped, and the egg exploded. He quickly found support for more experiments, and he spent the next 10 years developing this chance encounter into one of the most-used appliances in the world.

The microwave, Viagra, easy-open soda cans, Band-Aids, nylon, and X-rays were all, as legend has it, discovered by accident. Journalists and teachers are fond of tales of serendipity's grand role in the history of innovation, which is yet another example of the epiphany myth (see Chapter 1). The myth, in this form, is that innovation is random, and that people lucky enough to show up at the right place and at the right time reap rewards. The double-secret hidden message of these tales is that good things can happen to anyone—we're all created equally in our ability to have good fortune knock on our doors. But it's a deception: while serendipity has a starring role in innovation, it's what people do with the chance encounter that matters, and not the chance discovery itself.

In our everyday lives, we encounter odd moments when we see things beyond explanation. Our conditioned response is to ignore these moments or explain them away. We keep going on as planned and pretend we didn't see or think what we thought we did. Yet these moments, for the innovator, are the future knocking on the door. How else will new knowledge appear to us, if not as strange, bizarre, or incomprehensible experiences? (See Chapter 6.) The innovator's response has to be to chase these moments until curiosities are exhausted or new solutions are found, whichever comes first. But for most of us, even in one of these special moments, we fall back to the comfortable illusion that we already know everything there is to know. We forget that the common sense we hold dear today was, years or centuries ago, discovered by an innovative mind willing to ignore the common sense of her own time.

Innovation is always good

The chief cause of problems is solutions.

—Eric Sevareid[1]

In 1903, two crazy young men, without any engineering training or college education, built a machine the world told them couldn't be made. In the frigid 30-mile-per-hour winds of Kill Devil Hills, a few miles from Kitty Hawk, North Carolina, the Wright brothers made the first sustained powered flight with a person at the controls (see Figure 10-1). Orville won the coin toss and flew first, but the brothers took turns, making four flights before calling it a day. As amazing as their accomplishment was, it went unnoticed: five boys from the nearby village made up most of the crowd. Only two small newspapers bothered to report on the event because it was seen as a stunt, not a technological breakthrough. It's hard to believe, but the Wright brothers landed their plane on a not very interested planet. The world would have to wait another 30 years for the commercial aviation industry to begin.

Figure 10-1. An early Wright brothers' glider on a test run at the famed Kill Devil Hills.

But it wasn't the lack of interest in the development of powered flight that was the most curious thing: it was how the Wright brothers pitched their idea to potential investors. They didn't talk about multibillion-dollar industries, revolutionizing travel across the planet, or connecting people around the world. Instead, their pitch centered on the most ambitious idea in the history of civilization:

---

1 *http://www.museum.tv/archives/etv/S/htmlS/sevareideri/sevareideri.htm.*

the end of war.[2] They imagined that their small aircraft, in the hands of democratic governments, could be used to observe enemy movements from afar, rendering surprise attacks and violent conflicts useless.[3] The Wrights spent six years pitching their idea to the governments of the U.S., France, Germany, and Great Britain, eventually selling an aircraft to the U.S in 1909.

Despite the wonders the airplane delivered to civilization, revolutionizing travel, commerce, and communication, it must have been tragic for Orville Wright to live through not one, but two World Wars with significant and strategic roles for aircraft. WWII saw the German Blitzkrieg, the U.S. fire bombings of Dresden (where hundreds of thousands of civilians were killed), and the only wartime uses of atomic bombs in history, all horrific events made possible by airplanes born of the Wrights' design.[4] Airplanes revolutionized warfare, changing forever the power balance of world politics in favor of those with superior air forces. And as the terrorist attacks on New York City on September 11, 2001, revealed yet again, the uses of innovations like airplanes are impossible to predict.

In our religions, histories, and mythologies, we hold innovators to be great heroes, but we rarely speak their names when the downsides of their creations arise. In popular Greek mythology, the god Prometheus was loved for bringing fire to mankind, but shouldn't he also be partially accountable for the burning of Rome? Or, on a more personal level, if I gave you an apple pie that tasted good but later made you ill, wouldn't you complain? What if you bought a machine that saved you time but stained your clothes? Or a drink that doubled your efficiency but caused insomnia? It's overlooked by most, but some mythologies fear innovators; for example, Prometheus, who brought fire to mankind, was chained to a rock and tortured for eternity (see Figure 10-2). The men who

---

[2] http://www.archives.gov/publications/prologue/2003/winter/aero-conference-1. html.

[3] This belief in technology, particularly weaponry, as ending war, was shared by the inventors of dynamite and the submarine. Tesla also built war machines with this ideal in mind. The telegraph, television, the Internet, and even neural implants have been heralded with the same war-ending powers. An observer of history might note the problems that lead to war seem to have nothing to do with technology and much to do with human nature.

[4] Einstein, whose E=mc[2] played a pivotal role in the creation of nuclear weapons, agonized over the moral challenges involved with the use of his discoveries: http://www.amnh.org/exhibitions/einstein/peace/manhattan.php.

tried to build the Tower of Babel in the biblical book of Genesis were cursed and divided across the world.

Figure 10-2. *Rubens' famous painting* Prometheus Bound. *In the myth, Prometheus is chained to a rock, and every day an eagle comes and eats his liver, which regenerates by the next day. In most mythologies, there is a price for innovation. The subtitle of Mary Shelley's* Frankenstein *is "The Modern Prometheus."*

The invention of the airplane certainly worked out well, especially if your last name is Boeing or you're a pilot. But what if, instead, you are the railroad mogul ruined by air travel's rise, or a saintly mother of five who witnessed the destruction of your home by bombs dropped from airplanes? It's a different story. As we'll see, sorting out the meaning and impact of innovations is more complex than the task of making the innovations themselves.

Measuring innovation: the goodness scale

We all think we know what good is, but like all definitions, its shine fades when applied to real life. What might be good for you (finding a thousand dollars in your underwear or waking up on a

Maui beach) is probably bad for someone or something else (the person who lost the money, and the hapless sand crabs crushed beneath you). What we casually call *good* is rarely beneficial to everyone: it depends on who you are and where you stand. As Shakespeare's character Hamlet said, "There is nothing either good or bad, but thinking makes it so," and our diverse thinking on goodness is reflected by the 50 or more definitions for the word *good* offered by most dictionaries.

The same goes for innovation. Is an innovation good if it solves your problems or makes you money? Definitely. But what if it also causes people to lose their jobs? Or, as is more often the case, what if after people spend days learning to use the innovation, there is little benefit? Or their lives are more complicated? And then consider plastics, typewriters, and televisions, innovations that have brought many good things to the world. But what of the 2-liter soda bottles resting forever in landfills, the typewriters that were used to schedule trains to Auschwitz, or the millions of children watching hours of television in lieu of day care? Can we call these, and others like them, innovations because they're good in the largest sense? And, despite all the positive revolutions they've brought to the world, personal computers leave a wake of toxins and chemicals every time they're replaced by newer machines.[5]

There's no easy answer to this examination of innovation goodness, leaving plenty of room, much like the previous chapter, for the mythology of "all innovation is good" to survive. We have so much history with innovation as the driving force for our culture, economy, and psychology—from the cotton gin and Industrial Revolution to the personal computer and the Internet Age—that our confidence in innovation approximates a faith; when in doubt, innovate, despite the growing wave of unanswered questions about innovations past.

But there is at least one truth: all innovations have good and bad effects regardless of the intention of the innovator.[6] If we accept

---

[5] *http://www.greenpeace.org/international/news/green-electronics-guide-ewaste250806.*

[6] Certainly some creators can steer their creations one way or another. The inventor of a drug that cures stupidity or converts assholes into saints would be hard to criticize. Some inventors are agnostic about how their work is used, but in the cases of OXO Good Grips or prosthetic limb designers, there is definitely a goodness factor in how the thing itself is designed and the problems it intends to solve.

this, and concede that perspective is everything when it comes to goodness, we can reframe our judgment of innovations.

An innovation can be:

- **Good for you.** It earns you money, is enjoyable to work on, or solves a problem that interests you.
- **Good for others.** It provides income to help family and friends; solves problems for the poor, sick, or needy; or through the innovation, or profits generated from it, improves the lives of people other than you.
- **Good for an industry or economy.** It has benefits for many businesses and creates new opportunities for at least a subset of an industry or economy. Disruptions caused by the innovation are outweighed by new opportunities created.
- **Good for a society.** It has a net positive effect on a community, city, state, or nation. While there might be some negative uses of the innovation, the net effect is overwhelmingly positive. The innovation is designed for sustained value, not just short term. The innovator identified who it might be bad for and tried to minimize those effects.
- **Good for the world.** It has a net positive effect on the future of the human race.
- **Good for all time.** It doesn't sacrifice the long term for the short, benefiting not just this generation, but all future generations.

And we can also ask the twin questions:

- What problems does this innovation solve? Whose problems are they?
- What problems does this innovation create? Whose problems are they?

This list shows that many famous innovators can at best claim to have made things good for them, or good for corporations, with little value for others. (Having a large IPO or selling ideas for millions has debatable value on the goodness scale.) And many popular innovations—such as lightbulbs, automobiles, and computers—definitely benefit individuals and industries, but their contributions are tarnished by their negative environmental impacts. It gets complex quickly, but by framing the value of innovations on different perspectives, understanding innovation becomes possible.

The biases or self-interests that limit definitions of goodness are forced to surface.

Innovations are unpredictable (DDT, automobiles, and the Internet)

An illustrative tale of the challenge of goodness starts with a mix of chemicals, a Swiss scientist, and hordes of disease-carrying insects. In 1948, to the despair of mosquitoes everywhere, Paul Muller recognized the bug-killing properties of dichloro-diphenyl-trichloroethane, commonly known as DDT. This chemical was the first true pesticide in history and was used in enormous quantities during WWII to control the spread of typhus and malaria. It was so successful that in 1955 the World Health Organization (WHO), proudly armed with DDT, planned to eliminate malaria from the planet. The belief was that DDT's supreme potency, lasting for years in soil and weeks in water, could permanently eliminate disease-carrying insects in infested areas.

But the WHO soon observed strange things in places where DDT was used. Scientists realized that this new chemical had unexpected and complex collateral effects. The story went like this:

> The mosquitoes were effectively eliminated; however, roaches, less sensitive to DDT, survived, absorbing the poison. Small lizards happily ate the roaches. Those lizards developed nerve damage from the DDT (providing the widowed roaches with bittersweet glee), who, in their slow, near-drunken stupor, were easily consumed en masse by the local cat population. The cats, more sensitive to DDT than the lizards, died by the thousands, opening the door for an explosion in the rat population. And the kicker to the whole sordid tale is that the rats brought the threat of the plague to humans.[7]

For all their confidence, the technological leaders of the world were dumbfounded by the chain of events their actions put into play. At first, the WHO and many scientists refused to believe that

---

[7] This is a careful combination of several different accounts. There are many secondary reports that provide similar, and in some cases more dramatic, tellings of the events. See *http://catdrop.com/* compiled by Patrick T. O'Shaughnessy, professor of environmental health at the University of Iowa. The WHO itself isn't completely sure what did or did not happen, as expressed in their April 2005 staff newsletter: *http://www.who.int/formerstaff/publications/qn60.pdf.*

DDT could be responsible for everything they observed. It was unimaginable to the best scientific minds of the 1950s that one little chemical could cause so much damage. And since DDT was so new, and there were no mass uses of chemicals like DDT on record, everyone was ignorant of the possibilities. Much like the major innovations of the last decades—cell phones, wireless Internet, personal computers—DDT changed so much about how things worked that it was impossible to predict its impact, positive and negative, before it was used (see Figure 10-3).

Figure 10-3. DDT and airplanes were a perfect match. Here, DDT is being used on cattle to give them extra-special flavor.

Before DDT, people had little reason to fear pesticides or chemicals of any kind. It wasn't until Rachel Carson's book *Silent Spring* that people became aware of the negative impacts of DDT, and the modern environmental movement was born.[8] Beforehand, there was little public knowledge about the possibility of chemicals moving up the food chain, or the unpredictable nature

---

[8] There are still debates about the true risks of DDT, the Borneo tale, and whether the studies done of DDT on birds were accurate. Regardless of how much of this particular truth we surface, my point holds steady: all innovations have unpredictable effects, both good and bad. And often, as perhaps in the case of DDT, it takes a long time to understand the true impact of an innovation. See *http://reason.com/rb/rb061202.shtml*.

of shifting the species' balance in ecosystems. The scientific community did not understand the interconnectedness of ecologies and had little experience with the new kinds of chemicals they were producing. DDT's greatest value was its staying power, yet it was nearly impossible to predict that this very property would have intense destructive effects.

Other major innovations show similar patterns of diffusion with unexpected consequences arising as a result of successful adoption (see Table 10-1). Automobiles are one of the great successes of the early 20th century. They revolutionized society, enabling unprecedented commerce, travel, and leisure for the middle classes around the world. But their success has created many sizable, perhaps inescapable, problems; for example, over one million people are killed annually in automobile accidents (nearly 40,000 in the U.S. alone). Automobiles require expensive road development and upkeep, and they are major contributors to pollution.

Table 10-1. The two sides of innovations.

INNOVATION	GOOD EFFECTS	BAD EFFECTS
DDT	Controlled malaria, elevated living conditions in third-world nations, inspired professional-wrestling move[1]	Disturbed ecology, collateral species impact, DDT-resistant mosquitoes evolved
Automobile	Personalized transportation, empowered individuals, boosted commerce and urban development	Responsible for half of pollution in urban areas, 40,000 annual U.S. fatalities, and traffic; prompted urban sprawl[2]
Personal computers	Individual empowerment, communication, learning, the Internet	Rate of upgrades creates landfill, production creates hazardous materials[3]
Cell phones	Wireless communication, mobile access, convenience, portable emergency and safety system	Public annoyance, bad drivers become unguided missiles, that annoying person next to you in a restaurant

[1] *http://en.wikipedia.org/wiki/DDT_(professional_wrestling)*.

[2] WHO report, "Road safety: A public health issue," March 2004, *http://www.who.int/features/2004/road_safety/en/index.html*.

[3] *http://update.unu.edu/archive/issue31_5.htm*.

This is an essential paradox of innovation: no one knows, not even the inventors, how their creations will impact the world until they are used. Ford did not imagine pizza delivery boys. Ray Kroc didn't imagine epidemic obesity. Bill Gates and Steve Jobs did not consider software viruses. And Gutenberg, with all of his bibles, didn't envision *The Da Vinci Code*, nor the *New York Times* bestseller list it disgracefully (at least to him—he was a Catholic who printed bibles after all) dominated for months. For all the wishful thinking of innovators, innovations always have unintended consequences. They are free for use by others, and because everyone has different needs, values, ideas, and desires, there's no telling how the innovations born of one mind will be used by another.

A popular opinion held among inventors is that true breakthrough ideas are so different from our current thinking that we have no idea how to use them. This means that not only is the use of an innovation unpredictable after it has been accepted, but the time and motivation for its acceptance is unpredictable as well. Gordon Gould, one of the inventors of the laser, said:

> The triode...was invented in 1910, but it took years before a vacuum tube was ever sold commercially. Nobody knew what to do with them. They just knew that a triode provided a wonderful way to control a current with an electrical signal instead of a mechanical switch. Like the triode, the laser is also a very basic and important invention. But for the first five years or so of its life, there was a saying that the laser was "a solution in search of a problem."[9]

Many researchers take pride in this uncertainty, as it proves that they are as far out as possible in front of what we know, satisfying their drive to work in territory where breakthroughs are possible. But they downplay their lack of control, or their concerns, for how their discovery will be used. The intention of goodness doesn't bind the movement of ideas in any way. Barbed wire, designed to control cattle, which had innocent intentions (unless you're a cow), found its way into a pivotal role in WWI, limiting soldiers' movement across trenches and enabling some of the bloodiest warfare in the history of mankind.[10] Einstein's theory of

9 Kenneth A. Brown, *Inventors at Work: Interviews with 16 Notable American Inventors* (Microsoft Press, 1988).

10 *http://en.wikipedia.org/wiki/Trench_warfare*.

relativity revolutionized our understanding of the universe, but despite Einstein's initial disapproval, led to the atomic bomb. From every wonder comes a horror, and no one can claim certainty over what future the pursuit of an innovation will create.

In the late 1990s, the increased use of two innovations in finance—derivatives and CDOs—was a major contributor to the subprime crisis of 2007. As these ideas gained favor in the financial world, and banks of all sizes put an increasingly dangerous percentage of their assets in them, the stage was set for the greatest economic downturn since the Great Depression. Warren Buffett, Nassim Taleb (author of *The Black Swan*), and others pointed out the risks, but their voices were overwhelmed by those who believed that these innovations (unlike all innovations of the past) had no downsides. Even Alan Greenspan, Chairman of the Federal Reserve, had this to say about the derivative market in 1997: "Another far-reaching innovation is the technology of securitization—a form of derivative...[has] surely improved the efficiency of our financial markets." These new ideas were opening the door for more financial products that the experts and CEOs of banks invested in, despite not understanding how they worked.[11] No one is immune from wishful thinking, or hubris, when it comes to predicting the future. To be fair, the movement of innovation works the other way just as easily. Technologies developed for warfare—including the Jeep automobile, MedEvac helicopters, jet aircraft, and trench coats—often find important commercial, mass-market, and humanitarian uses.[12] Even the technologies used to develop the Internet originated in U.S. Government defense projects and with government funding. The lesson is that morality, or any philosophy, is invisible to the forces of innovation, and any innovator who takes his work seriously must operate with this in mind. What you do for good reasons may be used for bad, and what is done with bad motives can lead to good.

---

[11] The Greenspan quote, and the spirit of this paragraph, comes from Chapter 4 of *13 Bankers: The Wall Street Takeover and the Next Financial Meltdown*, by Simon Johnson and James Kwak (Pantheon, 2010), 106 (hardcover edition).

[12] *http://abcnews.go.com/GMA/Technology/story?id=1796227.*

Technology accelerates without discrimination

Imagine an innovation that cut your travel time to work in half. Impossible? One breakthrough of the 19th century was the clipper sailboat. Larger, faster, and more maneuverable, it reinvented cross-Atlantic trade and revolutionized the economies of entire nations. Until the 1830s, it took five weeks to make the crossing, but the clipper could do it in 12 days. It was a great innovation, accelerating many good things, but some bad ones as well.

In 1845, the Great Potato Famine began in Ireland, leading to the death of hundreds of thousands of people. It's believed that the potato fungus that destroyed Ireland's crops came from North America.[13] One theory is that the famine hadn't occurred sooner because the five-week journey across the Atlantic was long enough for the fungus to die in transit. However, with the shorter 12-day itinerary, it was only a matter of time before the fungus infested the clipper's destination.[14] There were other major causes, political and economical, but had the innovation of the clipper ship not taken place, the Great Famine might never have happened.

Most innovations have similar stories. Personal computers, which can be programmed to do anything, created the possibility of computer viruses. The Internet, designed to accelerate and distribute information, hastened the spread of those viruses, as well as spam, scams, and misinformation. Automobiles speed the police to crime scenes, but they also help thieves get away. The rising tide of technology raises all boats.

Instant messages and cell phone conversations are innovations in conveyance, as are many technological innovations. But they have no impact on the quality of the messages themselves, just as high-resolution television sets have zero effect on the quality of the acting or writing in the shows. Unless they're developing an innovation that motivates people to communicate more clearly or less selfishly, innovations that accelerate are unlikely to change the world in the way their creators expect. If you have someone good to talk to, and something important to talk about, communication

---

13 Historians are still sorting this out, but one report claims the infested potato came from Mexico: *http://www.pnas.org/cgi/content/abstract/91/24/11591*.

14 From *Diffusion of Innovations*, 452.

is rarely in need of acceleration. In fact, software that rewards people for slowing down and thinking about what they're reading and writing might be the greatest innovation of our time.

The good and bad, the future and the past

Where I grew up in New York City, sailboats were a mystery. My heart was with highways, subways, and rockets. On the days I'd happen to see a sail in Long Island Sound, I wondered why anyone would choose to travel slower than the latest technology allowed. But my opinion changed the first time I traveled on one. Standing in the shade of the sail, watching the smooth wooden bow rise with the waves, I felt the quiet power of the wind move me. Friends talked and calmly watched the sea, instead of wincing at the roar of engines and stink of diesel. The sails opened like wings, and we flew over the waves, the spines in the sail shining in engineered elegance, like the cable spans of the Brooklyn Bridge, providing an experience that no powerboat of any speed could ever replace.

Many innovations, for all their progress, leave behind a sailboat of forgotten goodness. And in our race to innovate, we instinctively reject people who hold on to the past, We discount the possibility that there is something timeless and good worth keeping, which our new idea might unintentionally eliminate. Is there an innovation that can replace a hug from your mom? Or an ice cream cone on a summer day? Is a strip mall a worthy substitute for an open meadow, or the latest Gehry office tower for the Chrysler Building? The passion of creation leaves us partially blind; we're focused so intently on what we're making that we forget the good things already here.

And while we laugh at groups who reject innovation as a concept— the Luddites, the Amish, or our technophobic friends—we are all just as resistant as they are, but in different ways. We follow conventions in our dress, speech, diets, and work schedules. We drive on the same side of the road, put socks on before our shoes, and eat dinner with knives and forks. Even the greatest innovators of all time, the big revolutionaries and radicals, followed the traditions of their day. No one innovates in all ways all the time; in fact, the biggest, baddest innovators in history followed more conventions than they broke.

As social creatures, we depend on traditions to form communities, governments, and families, and we believe these traditions are important enough to justify sacrificing our lives, or the lives of others, to protect them from change. And the grand irony is that all traditions, even religious ones, began as innovations. There was a day before men wore suits, and a time before Jews, Christians, and Muslims had their first holy texts (or the first churches to pray in). All of these ideas evolved into traditions over time, but only because people were, one day, willing (or forced) to try something new. There's a circular nature to innovation that's hard to see, but we're living inside it all the time.

The best philosophy of innovation is to accept both change and tradition and to avoid the traps of absolutes. As ridiculous as it is to accept all new ideas simply because they're new, it's equally silly to accept all traditions simply because they're traditions. Ideas new and old have their place in the future, and it's our job to put them there.

Epilogue: Beyond hype and history

Much of this book has told you what not to do and what not to think. The motivation was not to be mean, nor to do my impression of Statler and Waldorf, the two cranky guys locked in the balcony on *The Muppet Show*. Instead, it was to provide a baseline of truth to free you from the misguided yet common notions around innovation that run rampant in business and popular culture today. I consider your time on this planet to be precious, and I wanted to prevent you from aiming at false targets. There is so much hype around creativity today that the simple truths get lost in the noise.

So far, this book has been structured as a kind of history book, as history is the best available tool for sorting out how things in this world tend to happen. And if you're still here reading Chapter 11, history has done its job. But for this paperback edition, I want to do more than just point out what *not* to do. I want to leave you with the highest possible odds of success—however you define it.

When considering the creators of the great works of the past, it's surprising how few of them studied innovation or creative thinking. From van Gogh to Edison, Steve Jobs to Dave Eggers, almost none of them studied any of these topics in any conventional way. They didn't read innovation books, and they didn't take innovation classes. They miraculously overcame the frightening lack of TED videos and Malcolm Gladwell essays in their day, and found inspiration on their own. Many of them were dropouts or wanderers in the spaces between disciplines and professions. However, what they did do was pick specific problems they were passionate about, and got to work. They focused on those problems, often with little guarantee of reward. My point is that they didn't seem to need much understanding of innovation as an abstract concept, which many people today believe is the place to start. But a strong case can be made that the opposite is true. Many of the great figures didn't care to study; they preferred to *do*. They quickly got to work trying to solve important problems—that in some cases they thought they could profit from—and learned along the way.

Perhaps the greatest myth of all is that you need to be an expert in innovation in order to change the world.

Nikola Tesla, one of the inventors of radio,[1] and the man who made electricity in your home and office possible, didn't have the advantages of MBA programs, or the instant messages and WiFi Internet access his inventions would enable. Even George Westinghouse, the business mogul who financed much of Tesla's work, had no training in entrepreneurship or the theory of breakthrough inventions. Most progress throughout history was achieved by people working without the theories, resources, and devices we depend on today.

This is not a sales pitch for ignorance or becoming Amish; of course you should use any resource that helps you accomplish your goals. However, the toolkit you need is simpler than you think and depends less on tools or theories than on yourself. My intention in all these stories was first to reveal that the truth behind what these people actually accomplished was much more inspiring than the myths about them, and second, that the methods they used are simple and accessible to anyone. The challenge is that we have access to so much information today that it's easy to backslide into the faith that there is one magic answer out there, no matter how many times we're told, and even momentarily believe, there's not.

The human brain is fascinating for many reasons, but one of its most devastating features is its lust for wishful thinking. When faced with a day of avoidable hard work (e.g., work on a pet project that might lead to a breakthrough—or might not), our brains are amazingly fertile places for distraction. And a favorite kind of distraction is the quest for silver bullets. When we start looking for those silver bullets, we get distracted from the actual work and, before we know it, it's time for a meeting, dinner, or to go to bed. We postpone the only path that can give us what we want, namely, ordinary hard work, in favor of the wishful but impossible fantasy of finding a magic shortcut. Many people repeat the same failed cycle, convinced the failure is in their lack of knowing some secret, rather than their inability to put in the long, unavoidable hours required to fulfill their dreams.

---

[1] Just like we explored in Chapter 5, Tesla's claim of inventorship of radio depends on which elements you deem most important, including the filing of a patent. A good summary of the Marconi vs. Tesla patent history can be found here: *http://www.pbs.org/tesla/ll/ll_whoradio.html*.

A similar self-destructive pattern of behavior, which most of us share, is well described in *The Knowing-Doing Gap* by Jeffrey Pfeffer and Robert I. Sutton.[2] The book focuses on the wide gap between knowing how to do something and actually being able, or willing, to do it. You might know that to play a guitar you put one hand on the strings and hold a pick with the other, striking the pick against the strings to make noise. You've seen dozens of people do it, and you know what it looks and sounds like when it's done well. You might even know some related vocabulary, like riff or chord, which is a kind of knowledge. But the gap between that and the willingness to actually pick up a guitar with your own hands and play very badly for days, weeks, or months until your fingers learn to do the work is something else entirely.

The same is true when it comes to creativity, innovation, entrepreneurship, or anything else. We like to pretend that gap from knowing to doing is small, but it's enormous, and few people are willing to do the work to close that gap. It requires courage, persistence, comfort with risk, and a willingness to do work with no guaranteed external rewards. These qualities are more important than knowledge, degrees, or shelves of books on innovation. Reading a book on innovation is passive and safe. Putting the book down and starting a project is active and has risks. No matter how many books you read, this will never change.

Edison, Ford, Tesla, Gates, Jobs, and countless others could not pontificate about business and innovation theory half as well as any of the dozens of gurus you can find today, yet they accomplished infinitely more than those who have that "expertise." And although I have my name on patents and have worked successfully on projects making new things, I put myself in this camp as well. I make a living mostly for writing about things other people have done or are doing. In this age, being seen as an "expert" may have little bearing on the "expert's" ability to do the thing she is supposedly an expert in. This doesn't mean books are useless, but it does mean there's a paradox: the people most visible for being experts on innovation are those who spend more time writing and talking about it than actually doing it.

---

2 Jeffrey Pfeffer and Robert I. Sutton, *The Knowing-Doing Gap* (Harvard Business School Press, 2000).

The solution to these dangerous traps is simple: if you want to be creative, you must create things. If you want to be innovative, you must make things for other people. Just as if you want to be a guitar player, you should spend time every day actually playing guitar. End of story. It's only in the doing that you learn the best lessons. It's only in the specific act of trying to make something that solves some problem that whatever potential you have can manifest itself.

In his 2009 book *Outliers*, Malcolm Gladwell popularized the notion that it takes a person 10,000 hours of actually doing something to be good at it. It's a wonderfully simple notion. People come up to me often asking for advice, and I'll ask them, "How many hours have you spent trying to do it?" In the case of creative thinking and invention, often they reply, "Well, I haven't started yet," to which I say, "I doubt I can help you then." Until you are actively doing something, my advice isn't going to be of much use. If I'm shown a sketch for a design idea, I can comment. If you're stuck on a wicked problem, I can advise. But if you haven't committed any time to anything, there's very little I can do. Creativity is not abstract—it's specific. It shows up only when you are trying to do some particular thing. This seems obvious, but you'd be amazed by how many people never even take the first step toward whatever it is they dream about everyday. They've confused dreaming with doing, perhaps because the fantasy of doing it gives comforts and rewards that the reality might not.

Recently I had the honor of speaking at an event on innovation at UC Berkeley, organized by the *Economist*. I was honored to be on the same program as Jared Diamond, Robert Reich, Arianna Huffington, John Perry Barlow, and Ed Catmull (one of the founders of Pixar). The audience was packed with high-profile executives, government policy makers, and entrepreneurs. I was scheduled to speak on the second day, and I paid careful attention to everything said on the first. The word *innovation* was spoken 181 times that first day (I kept count), which was over 30 times an hour, yet I hadn't seen anyone do anything creative or innovative on stage. The conversation, however interesting, was about knowing. There was very little about doing. I chose to challenge this. What follows is an edited transcript of my speech:[3]

---

[3] A video and full transcript of the speech is available at *http://www.scottberkun.com/blog/2010/my-speech-at-the-economist/*.

Today I make a living as a writer of books, and I talk about ideas from those books. But my first career was leading teams of people. I worked on Internet Explorer in the early days of the Web, on versions 1.0 to 5.0, and my job was to be a practitioner in many of the things we've been talking about so far at this event. My job most of those years was to lead a team of designers and engineers in making new things. We did research, we made prototypes, we engineered those prototypes into products, and we released them into the world. We shipped a new version about every three or four months, and the work we did was relatively new in the world, or at least new for Microsoft.

When I quit my job in 2003 to write books, I knew I wanted to write a book about all the things I'd learned about creativity and invention—from personal experience and history—that I wished someone had told me when I started. There is so much misinformation in creative thinking and stories of invention. The book, The Myths of Innovation, is a bestseller and explains much of my success so far, and it's what I'm going to talk about today.

I'm an Occam's razor kind of guy. And Occam's razor is the notion that if you have two theories for explaining something, the simpler one is probably right. And when it comes to innovation, this is the lens I use. And with that in mind, I have a few observations.

First, most teams don't work. They don't trust each other. They are not led in a way that creates a culture where people feel trust. Think of most of your peers—how many do you trust? How many would you trust with a special, dangerous, or brilliant idea? I'd say, based on my experiences at many organizations, only one of every three teams, in all of the universe, has a culture of trust. Without trust, there is no collaboration. Without trust, ideas do not go anywhere, even if someone finds the courage to mention them at all.

Second, most managers/leaders are risk averse. This isn't their fault, as most people are risk averse. We have evolved to survive and that typically means being conservative and protecting the status quo. Looking at you in the audience, I can tell you I don't see anyone who has dressed innovatively or is behaving creatively right now. You are all sitting in nice little rows, dressed in nice, but conservative, business attire. This is not a surprise. Most people, most of the time, behave much as you are right now, certainly if anything involving work is concerned.

But without the ability to take risks, innovation and progress cannot happen. Even if you have a good idea, to bring it into the world is risky. Even if you can develop that idea into a good product, you must release it into the world, and there are a hundred unfair reasons outside of your control that will change how that ideas is perceived and whether it will succeed or fail. The history of innovation and progress of all kinds is made up mostly of failures for this reason, and any great successful revolution you hear of was almost certainly proposed and rejected many times before it found any support in the world at all. You'll find very few big ideas that were adopted with immediate open arms and unconditional love by those in power. We know this, which is why we often keep our best ideas to ourselves. They are much safer there.

Without teams of trust and good leaders who take risks, innovation rarely happens. You can have all the budget in the world, and resources, and gadgets, and theories, and S-curves, and it won't matter at all. Occam's razor suggests the main barriers to innovation are simple cultural things we overlook because we like to believe we're so advanced. But mostly, we're not.

Next, we need to get past our obsession with epiphany. You won't find any flash of insight in history that wasn't followed, or preceded, by years of hard work. Ideas are easy. They are cheap. Any creativity book or course will help you find more ideas. What's rare is the willingness to bet your reputation, career, or finances on your ideas—to commit fully to pursuing them. Ideas are abstractions. Executing and manifesting an idea in the world is something else entirely as there are constraints— political, financial, and technical—that the ideas we keep locked up in our minds never have to wrestle with. And this distinction is something no theory or book or degree can ever grant you. Conviction, like trust and willingness to take risks, is exceptionally rare. Part of the reason so much of innovation is driven by entrepreneurs and independents is that they are fully committed to their own ideas in ways most working people, including executives, are not.

Last, I need to talk about words. I'm a writer and a speaker, so words are my trade. But words are important, and possibly dangerous, for everyone. A fancy word I want to share is reification. *Reification is the confusion between the word for something and the thing itself. The word* innovation *is not itself an innovation. Words are cheap. You can put the word* innovation *on the back of a box, or in an advertisement, or even in the name of your company, but that does not make it so. Words like* radical, game-changing, breakthrough, *and* disruptive *are similarly used to suggest something in lieu of actually being it. You can say* innovative *as many times as you want, but it won't make you an innovator, nor make inventions, patents, or profits magically appear in your hands.*

I know from my studies if you are in the room when something that is later on called an innovation is being made, the language is always much simpler. Words like problem, solution, goal, experiment, and prototype—simple workman-like words—are the language you'll hear. And whenever I'm invited somewhere to talk about innovation, or to help an organization, and I'm in a meeting where any of the fancy words are used, I always raise my hand and ask, "What do you mean by innovation?" And most of the time they have to stop and think. They don't really know what they mean.

And if the person speaking doesn't know what they mean, odds are good no one else in the room knows what they mean either. Without good communication, trust is unlikely—if not impossible. Typically people mean one of five things when they say innovation: 1) We want to do something new. 2) We want something new and good. 3) We want something new and good and profitable. 4) We want to be more aggressive and work faster. 5) We just want to be perceived as being innovative. Any of these simple declarations are easy to understand. Odds of innovation happening go up when this kind of language pervades a culture, and history suggests clear language is one of the tools great thinkers, creators, and innovators have always used.

Lastly, thinking of Occam's razor, I'd love to know if you see a simpler way to understand how innovation happens than the one I offer in the book, and to let me know about it. And by the same token, if the book helps simplify how you think about what you do, or hope to achieve, I'd like to hear about that, too. Thanks for listening.

This speech outlines a simple plan. There is nothing fancy or new about this kind of advice, so many people dismiss it as too obvious. In fact, some people have dismissed this book for being too obvious. When tasked with thinking about their business, many executives and leaders hearing advice like mine look elsewhere. They assume, as perhaps you or your boss does, that they surely must need something more advanced and complex in order to do better work than what they're currently doing. But from the history I've studied, the organizations I've worked for, and the many companies I've visited, the opposite is true. It's the simple patterns and challenges that are ignored and discounted, and that fact more than any other explains much of the confusion and failure out there. But this advice does not seem "innovative," and since people somehow assume advice on innovation must itself be innovative, they dismiss it.

I'm certainly not alone in this simple view. While this perspective was in the minority of topics other speakers chose (and is an uncommon theme in popular business books: *Innovation and Entrepreneurship*, by Peter Drucker, is a notable exception), two others made similar points. Amy Edmondson, professor of management at Harvard University, was one of the few at the event thinking in terms of teams. She expressed how the pivotal role of collaboration, the "lack of interpersonal fear" as she describes it, plays in the team's ability to solve problems.[4] Her research has led her to believe the nature of good teams is more fragile and sensitive to the behavior of leaders than previously suspected.

Ed Catmull offered the wisest advice.[5] Despite Pixar's track record of 12 successful films (each earning more than $100 million), he offered a simple, humble view on his leadership role in these successes.

> We've got these successful things going on, and we misperceive how we got there or who the influences are. And we draw these wrong ideas and we then make a series of mistakes, which are not well grounded in reality. Which means the things that are happening now that are wrong at Pixar are already happening and I can't see them. And I have to start with that premise. And through all the history, there is something going on here and I don't know what it is.... Part of the behavior is I don't know the answers. And at first that seems a little bit glib. But after a while, people get that I really don't know the answer to a lot of these things. We discuss, we debate...and then we're very open and honest about the problems.

---

4 Amy Edmondson's research papers can be found at *http://hbswk.hbs.edu/faculty/aedmondson.html.*

5 The entire video of Catmull's speech can be found here, with text excerpts: *http://www.scottberkun.com/blog/2010/inside-pixars-leadership/.*

This is not what you typically hear from gurus. Instead of a five-step method or a "how-to guide for breakthroughs," he demonstrated his awareness of the unavoidable challenges this kind of work entails. If you are trying to do something amazing, something few others have done, you cannot be 100% certain of how to do it. And rather than hide this fact, he's decided admitting it is empowering, enabling him to trust others in the organization to participate in solving the problems they discover together. And if the president can behave this way, it invites all middle managers and employees to follow the same honest tactic themselves. All of which seems like simple, useful wisdom, until you consider how rare this kind of environment is. Many people talk about a culture like this, but talking about it and doing it are very different things.

But the biggest surprise was his stance on talented people who don't work well in teams. There is a myth in many organizations that the trade-off is worth it: if you have a rock star, you should tolerate his selfish, childish, destructive behavior. Catmull disagrees. He places the sense of trust in the team above any individual's abilities.

> [At Pixar] there is very high tolerance for eccentricity, [people are] very creative…to the point where some are strange…but there are a small number of people who are socially dysfunctional [and] very creative—we get rid of them. If we don't have a healthy group then it isn't going to work.

This is a simple idea, like many mentioned in this book, that some organizations are afraid to try. They violate this and other ideas because they assume their problems are too complex for these simple issues to be the cause. But in Catmull's view, the opposite is true: making a movie, a product, or a website requires many ideas from many different people, and only if the flow of ideas among people is healthy can the results turn out well. Having even one poisonous person around, no matter how talented she is, can render all other factors irrelevant—a point Robert I. Sutton focuses on in *The No Asshole Rule* (Business Plus, 2007). And the same is true for many of the myths that make up the majority of this book.

The simple plan

To connect many of these threads and others found earlier in the book, here is what I call *the simple plan*. If you picked up this book because you want to not only find ideas but bring them to reality, this is for you.

1. **Pick a project and start doing something.** It doesn't really matter what it is. You will need many experiences in trying to develop ideas into actual things before you get good at it. Don't wait around: make a website, start a blog, draft a plan. Get used to the fear you feel when starting something new, as well as the feeling of getting past that fear. Get paper and a pencil and make some lists of problems you'd like to solve, either at work, in your neighborhood, or in the world. Then choose one. Think about interesting ways to frame the problem (see Chapter 9). Until you start working on something, you won't truly start learning. And if you can't find a way to start a project at work, do it on weekends—history is full of innovators who never had their manager's approval to work on their ideas. There is always a way to start; just pick something small enough you can do yourself, or with a friend, and get to work.

2. **Forget innovation: focus on being good.** Most products out in the world are not very good. You rarely need a breakthrough to improve things, beat the competition, or help people suffering from a problem. If you carefully study the problem you're trying to solve, you will discover many clear ways to make it better. That's the best place to start. If you solve a problem for customers that makes them happy and earns you money, do you really think they will care whether it's innovative? They just want their problems solved. If you cured cancer conventionally, would patients refuse, saying, "But it's not innovative!" Of course not, so don't worry. Use the workman-like language of people who are later called innovators: *problem*, *prototype*, *experiment*, *design*, and *solution*, instead of the jargon of *breakthrough*, *radical*, *game-changing*, and *innovative*. This keeps you low to the ground, and prevents your ego from distracting you away from simply making good things.

3. **If you work with others, you need leadership and trust.** There's no point worrying about which innovation method you're using, or how much budget you're going to spend, if

people don't trust each other. It's the leader's job, as described in Chapter 7, to create an environment of trust so ideas can move freely and grow. It's also the leader's role to use his superior power to take risks, as well as protect the team from the dangers of those risks. This sounds obvious, but look around. It's rare. Many people do not trust their teams, nor work for leaders who are willing to stake their reputations on the risks of a new idea. It's uncommon to find someone in power who is not only willing to take the blame for problems, but also willing to give credit to subordinates as rewards for their efforts. If you're a leader, the burden is on you. If you're not, and you don't work for someone who creates trust and is willing to take risks, innovation will not happen where you are. You can quit, force the issue, or accept the status quo.

4. **If you work with others and things are not going well, make the team smaller.** There is a reason many inventions happen in small companies. In many large organizations, there are too many people involved for anything interesting to happen. The first advice I give teams when things are not going well is to kick people out of the room: reduce the number of people involved in making decisions. The dynamic of getting three people to agree to take a risk is dramatically simpler than getting 30 people to do the same. Three people will be fully invested and passionate about a decision in ways 30 people will never be. Another solution is to pick one creative leader and give her more power. A film director is the singular creative leader on a movie; yet most corporate or academic projects divide leadership across committees, diffusing authority, which always makes decisions more conservative—the opposite of what you want.

5. **Be happy about interesting "mistakes."** If you are doing something new, it cannot go well the first, second, or possibly fiftieth time. This is OK. Your mindset has to be "Am I learning anything from what I just did?" It might only be the lesson that the approach you tried won't work, but that's something you didn't know before. The more interesting the lesson, the better. You want to cultivate the mindset of an experimenter (see Chapter 3), asking questions about everything you make, and using the answers to those questions to fuel the subsequent attempts. Many people quit on their second or third try

for reasons that have nothing to do with history. There was not a story in this book where any of the brilliant minds mentioned succeeded on such a small number of tries. Perseverance, as simple a concept as it is, is rare.

It's difficult to stay focused on the simple plan. You'll dream of an easier way, ever hopeful for a trick or formula to avoid all the work and risks. But I hope that the stories you read earlier in this book will anchor your confidence and help this simple view stay with you. If you hold on to this book, you should have stories— based on fact—to refute many of the myths you'll frequently encounter in the world.

The following chapters provide advice on the three most essential challenges you'll face in trying to follow this simple plan: coming up with ideas, explaining them to others, and staying motivated after the initial thrill of a new project is gone. These chapters are based on essays originally published on my website, but they've been heavily revised for inclusion in this book.

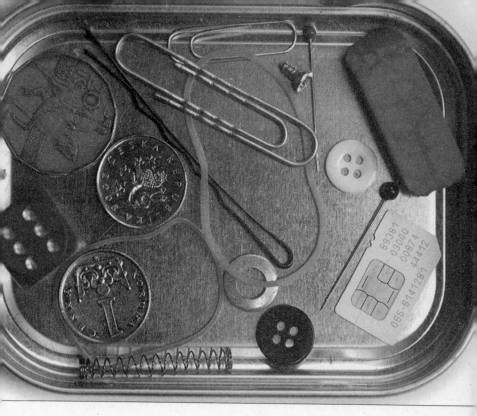

CHAPTER 12

Creative thinking hacks

Each one of us possesses everything necessary to be more creative. The problem is that schools, parents, and workplaces tend to reward us for following rules. It's something quite different to learn to ask our own questions and seek our own answers (which is one simple definition of creative thinking). This chapter is a high-speed, condensed version of a course I taught at the University of Washington on how anyone, with some honest effort, can easily become more creative at any task at any time.

Kill creative romance

Like most media today, this chapter starts with violence—and an unnecessary exclamation point! Close your eyes, and imagine the most amazing sword ever made. Now, with it in hand, attack every creative legend you've ever heard. (We've romanticized da Vinci, Mozart, and Einstein into gods, minimizing the ordinary aspects of their lives so intensely that their mothers wouldn't recognize them in the legends we tell.) Next, using your sword's mint-scented flamethrower attachment, set fire to childhood tales of Isaac Newton and the apple, Benjamin Franklin and the lightning kite, and Edison and the lightbulb. Think of other similar legends you've heard, even if they were not mentioned in this book. These popular tales of creativity are deceptive at best, wild lies at worst. They're shaped to placate the masses, not to inform or help people actually interested in doing creative work. Slash each and every one with your sword, throw a dozen napalm-coated hand grenades in for good measure, and watch your old, broken-down view of creativity go up in flames. Dance around the smoldering ruins! Roast marshmallows over the still-warm remains of your creative fulminations! The fun begins now: free yourself. Feel like you did when you were young, without any preconceptions over what is or is not creative.

In this new landscape, plant the following simple definition: *an idea is a combination of other ideas.* Say it five times out loud. Say it to your cat. Yell it out your car window at strangers waiting for the bus. Every amazing creative thing you've ever seen or idea you've ever heard can be broken down into smaller ideas that existed before. An automobile? An engine and wheels. A telephone? Electricity and sound. Reese's Peanut Butter Cups? Peanut butter and chocolate. All great creative ideas, inventions, and theories are composed of other ideas. Why should you care? Because if you want to be a creator instead of a consumer, you must view existing ideas as fuel for your mind. You must stop seeing them as objects or functional things—they are combinations of ingredients waiting to be reused.

Combinations

Cooking is a brilliant analogy for creativity: a chef's talents hinge on his ability to bring ingredients together to create things. Even the most inspired chef in history did not make bacon appear by mere concentration, nor suggest to the divine forces that a ripe tomato should be on the list of evolution's desired outcomes. Faith in the creativity-as-combinations view of the world helps creators in many ways. It means that if at any time you feel uncreative, the solution is to look more carefully at the combinations available to you, or to break apart something to see how it's made. Increasing creativeness doesn't require anything more than increasing your observations: become more aware of possible combinations. Here's a test: quickly pick two things in front of you, say, this book and your annoying, smelly friend Rupert. Now close your eyes and imagine different ways to combine them.

If you're stuck, here are three:

1. Rupert with a table of contents
2. An annoying, smelly book about innovation
3. Reading a book on, or making one out of, Rupert's face

Now while these combos might not be useful, good, or even practical, they're certainly creative (and if you think these are stupid and juvenile, you have confused bad taste with lack of creativity). Adding a third element, perhaps a gallon of cappuccino, might yield even more interesting combinations (a caffeine-overdosed, smelly book infused with Rupert's annoying personality).

Over time, creative masters learn to find, evaluate, and explore more combinations than other people. They get better at guessing which combinations will be more interesting, so their odds improve. They also learn there are reusable combinations, or patterns, that can be used again and again to develop new ideas or modify existing ones. For example, musicians throughout history have reused melodies, chord progressions, and even entire song structures. The national anthem of the United States was based on the tune of an old British drinking song.[1] The Disney film *The Lion King* is a retelling of Shakespeare's *Hamlet*. Shakespeare was likely influenced by the early Greek tragedies. Study any creative field, from comedy to cooking to writing, and you'll discover patterns of reuse and recombination everywhere. It's an illusion that when an artist makes a painting or an author writes a novel it appeared magically into her hands from out of nowhere. Everything comes from somewhere, no matter how amazing or wonderful the thing is. The *Mona Lisa* was not the first portrait any more than the Destiny's Child song "Survivor" was the first four-minute R&B hit.

I'm not suggesting you steal something someone else made and put your name on it. That's theft, and a fairly uncreative kind of theft at that. Instead, the goal is to recognize how much in the world there is to borrow from, reuse, reinterpret, use as inspiration, or recombine without breaking laws or violating trust. Every field has its own rules and limitations, but creative fields are more liberal than you'd expect.[2]

Inhibition

We're afraid. We're afraid of the dark, of our parents, and what our parents do in the dark. Our tiny, efficient brains do their best to keep us from thinking about things we fear or don't understand. This is good for survival but bad for combination making. We shut down the pursuit of many combinations because of predictions we make about what the result will be. But remember: we suck at prediction. Lewis Thomas (see Chapter 7) mentioned the best sign of progress in his research lab was laughter, and laughter often comes from surprise.

Many of us who have the potential to be creative fail only because we struggle to turn off our filters and fears. We don't want to do anything that could yield an unexpected result. We seek external

---

1 *http://en.wikipedia.org/wiki/The_Star-Spangled_Banner.*

2 An interesting challenge to this claim is the issue of sampling in music. How much of one song can another artist sample and reuse? One second? Five? None? See the excellent film *Copyright Criminals*, which explores this question from many different perspectives (and there's lots of good music in the film, too): *http://www. pbs.org/independentlens/copyright-criminals/film.html.*

validation from our teachers, bosses, family, etc., but creativity usually depends on internal validation. We have to judge for ourselves whether our ideas are interesting or useful.

One way to think of creative people is that they have more control over their fears—or less fear of embarrassment. They're not necessarily smarter or more capable of coming up with good ideas, they simply filter out fewer ideas than the rest of us. Creativity has more to do with being fearless than intelligent or any other adjective superficially associated with it. This explains why many people feel more creative when drinking, on drugs, or late at night: these are all times when their inhibitions are lower, or at least altered, and they allow themselves to see more combinations of things than they do normally.

Environment

Creativity is personal. No book or expert can dictate how you can be more creative. You have to spend time paying attention to yourself: when do ideas come easiest to you? Are you alone? With friends? In a bar? At the beach? Are there times of day when you're most relaxed? Is there music playing? Start paying attention to your rhythms and then construct your creative activities around them. To get all Emersonian on you, this is called self-knowledge:[3] you can't be productive as a creator if you're not paying attention to your own behavior and learning how best to cultivate the unique wonder in this universe that is you. Nothing is more counterintuitive than trying to be yourself by being like other people. It doesn't work that way—no book, course, or teacher can give this to you.

To help you figure this out, you need to experience different ways of working, and pay attention to which ones best suit you. They might be unexpected, not fitting into your framework (i.e., filters) for how creative work should be done, or what's appropriate for a 42-year-old middle manager to do. I learned that I tend to be most creative late at night. I don't find it convenient, and neither does my family, but I've recognized it to be true. If I want to maximize my creativity, I will spend hours working late at night. Each of us

---

[3] Read Ralph Waldo Emerson's essay "Self-Reliance" at *http://www. emersoncentral.com/selfreliance.htm.*

responds to environmental conditions differently. Half the challenge is experimenting to find out which ones work best; the other half is honoring them despite how inconvenient or unexpected they might be.

Persistence

Being creative for kicks is easy. But if you want to be creative on demand you must develop helpful habits, and that's about persistence. You won't always find interesting combinations for a problem right away, and identifying fears and working through them is rarely fun. At some point, all creative tasks become work. The interesting and fun challenges fade, and the ordinary, boring, inglorious work necessary to bring the idea to the world becomes the reality. Study the histories of great creators, and you'll find a common core of willpower and commitment as their driving force. Van Gogh, Michelangelo, and Mozart worked every day. Edison, Hemingway, and Beethoven, as well as most legendary talents, outworked their peers. Forget brilliance or genetics, the biggest difference between the greats and us was their dedication to their craft. Each of the names we know had peers who were just as talented, or more so, but twice as lazy. They consistently gave up before their projects were finished. Want to guess why we don't know their names? The world can only care about ideas that are shared.

When I give lectures on creative thinking, I often ask who in the audience has had an idea for a business, movie, or book. Most of the audience raises their hands. I then ask how many people have done any work at all on these ideas, and most of the audience drops their hands. That tells the whole story: ideas are lazy. They don't do anything on their own. If you aren't willing to do the ordinary work to make the idea real, the problem isn't about creativity at all.

When an idea is fully formed in your head, there's no escaping the fact that for the idea to change the world, it has to leave your brain—a journey that only happens with hard work and dedication. Writing proposals, sketching designs, pitching ideas: it's all work you know how to do. But how far are you actually willing to go to make your idea real?

Creative thinking hacks

Here are some clever tactics for applying this advice:

- **Start an idea journal.** Write down any idea that pops in your mind at any time. Don't be inhibited: anything goes. You will never have to show anyone else this journal, so there should be no filters—it's safe from judgment. This should help you find your own creative rhythms, as over time you can note what times of day you're more creative. I recommend a paper journal so you can doodle and write freely, but digital journals also work. Whenever you're stuck, flip through your journal. You're bound to find an old idea you've forgotten about that can be used toward the problem you're trying to solve.

- **Give your subconscious a chance.** The reason ideas come to you in the shower is that you're relaxed enough for your subconscious to surface ideas. Make this easier: find time to turn your mind off. Run, swim, bike, have sex, do something that's as far from your creative problem as possible. Afterward, you might just find that the problem you struggled with all morning isn't as hard, or that you have a new idea for approaching it.

- **Use your body to help your mind.** This is entirely counterintuitive to your logical mind, but that's exactly why it's so likely to work. In John Medina's *Brain Rules*, he explains how physical activity, even for people who don't like it, has positive effects on brain function. The theory is that for most of our evolutionary history, the acts of physical exertion and maximum brain function were correlated (think how creative you have to be when being chased by tigers). If your body is active, your mind will follow. Einstein and Bohr used to debate physics while going for long walks—they both believed they thought better when moving around. This might be true for you.

- **Inversion.** If you're stuck, come up with ideas for the opposite of what you want. If your goal was to design the best website for your team, switch to designing the worst one you can imagine. Five minutes at an inverted problem will get your frustrations out, make you laugh, and likely get you past your fears. Odds are high you'll hit something so horribly bad that it's interesting, and in studying it, you'll discover good ideas you would never have found any other way.

- **Switch modes.** Everyone has a dominant way of expressing ideas: sketching, writing, talking. If you switch the mode you're working in, different ideas are easier to find, and your understanding of a particular problem will change. This is both a way to find new ideas and to explore an idea you're focused on. Working on paper, rather than computers, can make this easier because you can doodle in the margins (a form of mode switching), something you can't really do with a mouse and a keyboard. Or, try explaining your problem to a child, or to the smartest person you know, which will force you to describe and think about the problem differently.

- **Take an improvisational comedy class.** This will be easier and less painful than you think. These classes, offered for ordinary people by most improv comedy groups, are structured around simple games. You show up, play some games, and slowly each week you learn how to pay more attention to the situations the games put you in, as well as how to respond to them. You will eventually become more comfortable with investing in combinations without being sure of the outcome.

- **Find a partner.** Some people are most creative when they're with creative friends. Partnering up on a project, or even being around other creative people who are working on solo projects, keeps energy levels high. They will bring a new perspective to your ideas, and you will bring a new perspective to theirs. It also gives you a drinking buddy when things go sour.

- **Stop reading and start doing.** The word *create* is a verb. Be active. Go make things. Make dinner, make a drawing, make a fire, make some noise, but make. If all your attempts at being creative consist of passively consuming, no matter how brilliant what you consume is, you'll always be a consumer, not a creator. An entire culture of tinkerers and makers is out there, with projects and tools to help you get started. Check out *http://makezine.com* and *www.readymade.com*, two sites waiting to show you the way.

CHAPTER 13

How to pitch an idea

Pitching is for the powerless. You don't pitch unless you need something from someone else, whether it's money for a start-up or permission to go out on a date. If you put yourself into a position where you need to pitch to get what you want, don't mess it up by pretending you are in control. You're not. You are asking, and if you want to get what you are asking for, you must prepare. The goal is to make it as easy as possible for someone to say yes, and that doesn't happen all on its own. Chapter 4 was about how there has never been an idea that sold itself. In my experience, the skill most deficient among people with good ideas is the ability to persuade others on the merits of those ideas. In this chapter, I'll provide you with a simple way to think about pitching that will dramatically improve your chances.

The act of bringing an idea to someone who has resources you need is called a pitch: movie screenplays, business plans, or just about anything you might call an idea is pitched from one person to another. And although the industries may differ, the basic skill is the same.

All ideas demand change

By definition, acting on an idea means something different will take place in the universe. Even if your idea is undeniably brilliant, it will force someone, somewhere, to change something. Most people do not like change—they fear it. And the qualities of your idea that you find so appealing may be precisely what make your idea so difficult for others to accept. Galileo was certainly proud of his contributions in proving the sun was at the center of the solar system, but his hubris, and lack of interest in explaining it in terms palatable to the Church, made him and his theory unpopular. So, many people who have big ideas, surprised by outside resistance to their ideas, become frustrated. And that frustration makes their pitches worse, making it less and less likely others will ever accept their ideas.

When you, as a creator, put your great idea in front of someone who does not want change, you and your idea are at a disadvantage because the answer will generally be no. So before you pitch, you must study the innovators of the past and be prepared to face the common kinds of rejections (see "Idea killers" on page 90). It's also worth seeking out people interested in change, or who you know have a clear need or problem your idea can satisfy. Then you're not talking about you and your idea, you'll be presenting a possible solution to their problem. The healthy cultures described in Chapter 7 pitch ideas and make changes much more easily than stagnant, struggling organizations. Wise leaders usually depend on change, and not only encourage positive change to happen, but expect people at all levels of the organization to contribute. It requires maturity for these managers to make this kind of environment successful, but when they pull it off, smart people are systematically encouraged to be smart. But no matter who you work with, the burden of developing a good pitch falls heavily on the creative person's shoulders. The following steps provide you with suggestions for developing and presenting an effective pitch.

Step 1: Refine your idea

The classic mistake of would-be idea pitchers is to present the idea well before it's ready. When most people find an interesting idea, their egos quickly seduce them into doing silly and nonproductive things, like annoying everyone they come in contact with by telling them how amazing their new idea is.

The thrill of being clever is so strong that they forget:

1. There are thousands of good ideas bouncing around.

2. People rarely think about their ideas thoroughly enough to recognize why no one has executed on them before.

3. They have to put together the plans, skills, and thinking required to deliver the ideas to the world before anyone will take them seriously.

So, to present a good pitch, you must think about execution and delivery. Saying "We should build cars that go 1,000 miles per hour and get 100 miles per gallon that easily fold to fit in your back pocket," and "We should make a children's movie that is funny and intelligent for parents and children, but also has a positive spiritual and moral message" count as interesting ideas. They're good starts. But they won't be pitchable ideas until there's a detailed proposal for converting the abstract idea ("build a breakthrough automobile") into tangible and realistic plans ("the trans-warp drive I've already designed improves gasoline efficiency tenfold").

Until the concepts and hard parts are fleshed out enough to demonstrate that the spirit of an idea is matched with specifics, it doesn't have much of a foundation, and the pitch is bound to fail. People can dismiss it quickly just by asking two or three basic questions. Always remember that moving from an interesting but vague idea to a specific and actionable plan is difficult. Getting feedback on a hunch or vague idea is fine provided you have a friend who is a sounding board and doesn't feel like you're wasting his time. But don't take your pitch to your boss or a potential investor until you're able to answer some basic questions, such as:

- What problem does this solve?
- Whose problem is this? Is it important to them? Is there evidence they'd pay to have it solved?
- What are the toughest challenges implied by the idea? How will you solve each one?
- Do you have a prototype, sample, or demonstration (aka proof of concept)? Of the remaining work, what is hardest to do?
- Why are you the right person to solve this?
- Why should our organization give you money/support/time to work on this?

These are the kinds of questions someone who gets pitched to on a daily basis (say, the author of a book about innovation) is likely to ask; therefore, a good pitcher will have done more than superficial thinking on her answers, especially if she believes the person listening is important enough that she'll only get one shot to pitch her idea. And as she prepares the pitch, keeping these questions in mind, her thinking about the idea will improve dramatically, and she'll have discovered many important nuances, traps, and possibilities that the person hearing the pitch would likely mention.

Step 2: Shape your pitch

Big ideas require more changes to take place, and all things equal, this means the pitch must be more thorough. Convincing a CEO to start a new million-dollar project will take more effort than convincing your best friend to loan you his pen. First, assess the scope of your idea, from narrow to grand. Is it:

- A modification to something already in existence?
- A new feature or enhancement to an existing product/website/company?
- A major new area of an existing product/website/company?
- An entirely new but small and simple project?
- An entirely new but large and possibly complex project?
- An organizational, directional, or philosophical change to an existing organization?
- A new organization?
- A new nation, planet, or dimension (sorry, but you'll have to look elsewhere for help petitioning the omnipotent forces that run the universe)?

When you've identified the scope, research how others pitching ideas of similar scope went about it. Find out what they did, and whether they were successful—if they weren't, learn from their mistakes. There are books about pitching business plans, movie scripts, and even pitching yourself (e.g., job interviewing, dating). Do your homework: know some of the basic strategies or industry expectations for the kind of pitch you're doing. I can't list them here, since they vary from industry to industry, but an easy way to have your great idea ignored is not to do the legwork to find out what the format of pitches in your field tends to be like.

Step 3: Follow the power

Make a list of the people who are potential recipients of your pitch (aka catchers). This could be your boss, the VP, another company, a bank, a publisher, who knows. Base this list on two criteria: who you might have access to, and who has the power needed to implement the idea. Here's a rough guide, ordered from fantastic to depressing, of who has the power you need:

- You
- A friend or peer in your organization
- Your boss
- Someone above your boss in the organization
- Someone you know in another organization
- Someone you don't know and don't have easy access to
- You're not sure who has the power

You're not sure who has the power, and you realize you are currently paralyzed on a cold, wet basement floor, and a shifty-looking squirrel is poking you in the ribs with a sharpened pencil (see, it can always be worse). If you don't know who to pitch to, ask around. There's little sense developing your pitch if there's no one to catch it. If you don't have access to the person with the power you need, make a list of who has access to them, working backward until you can list people you actually know. You may need to work through this network, making several pitches, before achieving the results you want. Just getting to the real pitch situation may take days, weeks, or months of preparation and pitching to the wrong people. This demoralizes the idealists, who often say, "My idea is so great, why should I have to go through all this?" The reason is simple: people are bad judges of their own ideas. All the others who claimed to have great ideas, but didn't, sufficiently annoyed those with power enough that they added extra legwork to filter out people. The people who are truly passionate will do it; those who merely claim to believe in their ideas won't.

Step 4: Start with their perspective

Put your pitch aside. Imagine you have mind-melded with the person to whom you are pitching. How does she think about the world? What kinds of things is she probably interested in? What is her typical day like? How many unsolicited pitches does she receive a day? Consider her view of the world and keep it in mind while developing your pitch. The better your pitch fits into her needs, the greater your odds of being successful, or even being listened to for more than 30 seconds. This doesn't mean you should sell out or create ideas that you think only a specific person will like. Instead, you have to be aware of how your perspectives differ, and improve your ideas—and how you communicate them—based on that awareness. This may help you decide who to bring your pitch to: the most powerful person in the organization might share none of your philosophy, but the third or fourth most powerful person might. The latter is going to be a better place to start.

If the best person to pitch to is someone you know, start paying attention to how he handles pitches from other people. Have you ever seen him say yes to a suggestion? There are people in this world who never say yes, in which case your odds are quite long for reasons that have nothing to do with you or your idea. Others are only convinced by data and won't start listening until there are some numbers to look at. Some need to hear a well-told and relevant story that illustrates the problem. People are so different in their preferences that the more you can learn about the person you're pitching to, and study the pitches he's previously approved, the better your odds are going to be.

Step 5: Make three pitches

Always prepare three versions of your pitch: 5 seconds, 30 seconds, and 5 minutes.[1] The five-second version, also known as the elevator pitch, is the most concise single-sentence formulation of your idea. Refine, refine, refine your thinking until you can say something intelligent and interesting in a short sentence. Practice your pitch on friends, peers, or strangers by giving the five-second version, and then asking them to help you refine it again. "My idea? It's a way to make car engines twice as efficient and five times as powerful." This can be done for any idea: never allow yourself to believe yours is so complicated and amazing that it's impossible to explain in a sentence. If you were to give me this excuse, I'd tell you it means you have not yet worked hard enough on your idea to understand how to express it in simple terms.

As proof, here's a list of diverse and complex ideas and a simple five-second explanation for each.

Discovering DNA

"I'm working to explain how human cells reproduce."

Inventing lightbulbs

"I'm making light from electricity."

Writing a brilliant novel

"The story explores 20-something angst in the Digital Age."

Improving antilock brake algorithms

"I'm making cars safer to drive."

The 30-second and 5-minute versions should grow naturally out of the 5-second version. In 30 seconds, there's time to talk about

---

1 Ari Blenkhorn suggested this breakdown to me years ago.

how you'll achieve what you described, or provide specifics for the two or three most significant things people will want to know if they thought the 5-second version was good. If you can't distill what you're doing in 5 and 30 seconds, don't worry about the 5-minute version: odds are you'll never be able to get anyone to listen for that long. However, since some people prefer written proposals for pitches, this gives you a chance to deliver the 5-second, 30-second, and 5-minute versions all at once. In this case, it's often best to keep the same structure. Start with your shortest pitch, then provide the next level of detail, and, finally, provide a point-by-point detailing of how, given the money and resources you need, you'll achieve what you described in the first sentence (the five-second pitch). Remember, you won't have all your materials with you when pitching ideas. So, at least briefly consider how you would deal with the different tools available in the following situations:

- The elevator: it's just you and your mind
- The slow elevator: you, and maybe something to show from your pockets
- The lunch: you, and maybe something to show, napkins to draw on, alcohol
- The executive review: you, your laptop, slides, prepared handouts, yes men, splunge men[2]

Sometimes it can be to your advantage to pitch with a partner. If you can find a partner who complements your skills, and with whom you can happily collaborate, it's worth it (and though your ego may try to convince you you're better off alone, you probably aren't). It doubles your network of organizational connections, your idea benefits from having two minds thinking about it, and you'll have at least one ally in the room with you.

Step 6: Test the pitch

The longer you spend with an idea, the more vulnerable you are to your ego. Get out of your office, cubicle, or apartment, and find smart, honest people who will give you feedback. Ask them to

---

2 The word *splunge* means "I'm saying yes but I'm not a yes man." If you've never heard the word splunge before, and you spend time in meetings, you owe it to yourself to watch the splunge scene from episode 6 of *Monty Python's Flying Circus*.

pretend they are whomever it is you plan to pitch to (this can be fun if they behave like Bill Gates, Donald Trump, Machiavelli, Ozzy Osbourne, or a caricature of your boss). Then go through your pitch, responding to their questions (or ignoring their laughter). You won't always get the feedback you want, but you'll sharpen both your idea and the way you talk about it. From your practice pitches, develop a list of questions you expect to be asked during the pitch, and prepare to answer them. Then do it again and again.

Step 7: Deliver (a pitch is a performance)

There are three kinds of people who are rare in this world:

- Those who are excellent communicators
- Those who find interesting and useful ideas
- Those who can convert an idea into a realistic plan

It's exceptionally rare for one person to be good at all three. If you think it's you, you're probably wrong. Get some honest feedback from people who are not your parents before putting any faith in this belief.

Even for those lucky enough to have all three sets of skills, a pitch is a kind of performance. It is done live, in real time, in front of other people. Performing requires practice—and not just at the level of testing described earlier. There are many nuances, like eye contact, tone of voice, and ability to convey conviction, that you can't get a sense of without putting in many hours of doing it for real. And if you do put in the time, there is always the risk of coming off as phony, like Vince, the ShamWow guy of infomercial fame. Too much polish and perfection can work against you. Practice and listening to feedback is your best ally, but sadly there is no magic formula for getting it just right. The people who offer one, or who rely on tricks and manipulations for pitching, are those who haven't worked to understand their audience well or don't believe in what they're pitching.

The best delivery advice I can offer is to make sure you prepare for a positive response. What happens if they say, "That's interesting. What do you want from me?" Do you want money? A team of people? A meeting with executives? A commitment from them to review a longer proposal? Know what you need, mentally prepare the sequence of steps, and be ready to ask for it. If there are other people involved whose approval you'll need, ask them to set up a meeting for you. If there is a form that needs to be filled out, make sure you have one with you. If you've just pitched to someone you cornered in an elevator, simply ask for the privilege to email her later.

Step 8: Learn from failure

It never surprises me how many people expect their first pitch, for their first big idea, to get them what they want. Most pitches fail. Most businesses fail. And most successful creative people, including entrepreneurs, pitch their ideas dozens of times before getting a single bite. And after they get the funding or support they need, when their idea becomes real, they still have to promote it to the world, which is really just another kind of pitching. This is the burden of the innovator: if you want to make something new, dozens of less-than-fun things come along for the ride. This means when things don't go well, don't waste time complaining about unfairness, because actually it's quite fair in some sense. Everyone gets ideas rejected no matter how good or bad the ideas are. No one is immune. The most useful thing to do is to convert what happened into a learning experience. Don't just plod on repeating the same mistakes again and again. Spend time debriefing on what went well, what didn't, and what you can learn.

Never go to bed after a failed pitch without an understanding of what went wrong. Which points didn't they agree with? Where did they cut you off? Which assumptions did they refute? You might learn there are criteria for green-lighting ideas you didn't know about. It's possible they objected to something about your approach: maybe they didn't appreciate you accosting them during lunch, waving a stack of handouts in their faces. If someone else in the room was observing the pitch, ask for his feedback. In short, maximize the value from completed pitches. Recoup your investment. Do everything you can to make the next pitch better than the previous. And never hesitate to go back to your idea and use what you've learned from your pitches to make not just the pitch, but the idea itself, better than it was before. From a tactical perspective: ask, "To whom else can I give this pitch?"

Every organization's hierarchy has lots of people at peer levels. Would any of them be interested? Go back to your list from step 3. Consider compromising on how much power is needed to make your idea happen, or how to split your idea into smaller ideas. Maybe focus on the first small piece of your larger idea, and revisit the rest after you've had some initial success.

Step 9: Go your own way

In every creative pursuit, there are people rejected by "the system" who went off on their own, scraped together their own resources, and made amazing things happen. Low-budget films like *Napoleon Dynamite*, *Clerks*, and *Pi* happened only because a small group of people believed enough in their ideas to make the sacrifices and do it themselves. Many of the famous corporations mentioned in this book began as self-owned, independent operations. Today, books and novels can be self-published more easily than ever. Businesses, especially those on the Web, can be founded on small-business loans or second mortgages. There is always a way to do it if your ideas sufficiently compel you to take risks and make use of your own time. This will likely demand that you reduce the size of your ambitions, but so what? It was bound to happen anyway, even if someone granted you all the resources you needed. But if you do it yourself, *you* are in control of all the things you care so much about—you're not obligated to heed the opinions of someone whose passions likely diverge from yours. When asking for money, nothing looks better on your resume than having the experience of doing similar projects entirely at your own expense. And nothing is more likely to give you personal satisfaction than completing work where every decision was free of the compromises that come with borrowing money from other people. There is always a way to achieve a dream—if you are creative enough to find it.

How to stay motivated

All great tasks test our motivation. It's easy to court ideas over beers and change the world with rough sketches on the backs of napkins. But like most things taken home from bars, new challenges arise the next day. It's in the morning light when work begins, and grand ideas become more complex than they seemed hours before. Doing interesting things in this world requires effort, and it's no surprise we often abandon our passions for simpler, more predictable things. Although we like to talk about talent—that callow, overrated, but useful bastard—it can't do anything for us if it's locked in the basement by our ever-flighty motivations. Achievement demands discovering personal motivations and learning to use them. The masters in all fields are foremost great self-manipulators, orchestrating their will to achieve what the rest of us cannot (or will not). However, there is no true handbook for motivation—only a treasure map of landmarks and a handful of bones to roll.

The big motivations

These are the ones I've found in myself and in some of the notable legends mentioned earlier in this book. If these factors hit home, I hope you kick much ass. But if they fail you, think about what's missing and you'll be on your way to discovering what works for you.

Anger

What pisses you off? What is wrong in the world, in your community, in your workplace, in your family, and what are you doing about it? Or will you just sit there and pretend, for another week, another year—like other people do—that it's all OK? When are you going to use your frustration as fuel for doing something, anything, that brings the world a little closer to right? And don't just vent: convert rage into possibility. Use exhaust from one system to drive another. Recycle negative energy, whether it's criticism, judgment, or competition, even if it comes from your own heart, and shape into something of unmistakable goodness.

Necessity/suck it up

All great ideas require grunt work. Van Gogh mixed his own paints. Michelangelo cut his own marble. If you chicken out

because you don't want to get your hands dirty, know that you
are putting yourself in not-very-worthy company. Sometimes the
only way to discover, to grow, to make something great is through
learning the basic, the trivial, the mundane: sufficient repetition
grants mastery of anything. Learning to draw, sing, or dance is a
slow process of tiny, trivial increases in skill. A boring task might
be required before you can attempt an amazingly cool challenge.
Beethoven and Mozart practiced scales just like everyone else, so
don't cry when it comes time to do yours. Or get clever: find a
partner willing to be paid for the grunt work you hate, or who
desires to witness the wrangling of the big ideas you love.

Crazy necessity

Deliberately put yourself in situations where you have no way out
but through. Sign a book deal, quit your job to make that film,
buy a one-way ticket to somewhere no one you know has ever
gone. While it's not advisable to gamble your life if you have
dependents (a spouse, children, or your loving cat, Blinky), you'd
be surprised how much support you can get for crazy necessity if
you enlist it from loved ones, especially if you've been there for
them. If you don't ask, or never get crazy in any way at any time,
you're the only one to blame: no one else can commit to one of
your ideas but you. Yes, it's true you don't know what's on the
other side, but that's exactly the reason to pursue it.

Pride

Prove people wrong. They say it can't be done? Do it. They tell
you it's a waste of time? Waste away. Never let anyone define for
you who to be, how to use your time, or what you are capable of.
Turn that naysayer into a competitive guidepost, recasting every
doubting Thomas into a secret twisted cheerleader. But don't
focus on their critical words—use them as ammunition. Take their
judgment, harness it to your pride, and ride them like a team of
horses past the fools, over the hills, and toward your dream. Have
no critics? Set a goal for yourself you're not sure you can meet.
Write it down, sign it, post it on your bedroom wall, show it to
friends and family so there's no way to sneak out the back door.

Death

If you want the most mileage out of this lifetime, behave as if it's the only one you get. Henry Rollins said, "We have infinite potential but finite time," and he meant that you can't do everything, but if you choose wisely, you can do any one thing you want. Perhaps that thing won't be done as well as you'd like or earn you a living, but it can be yours in some form if you're motivated to have it before you die. Once a week, imagine being on your deathbed (it can be fun: think Mexican Day of the Dead). Ask yourself: what will I regret not having done if I knew I was going to die today? Make a list and get to work. Otherwise, you deserve all your dying regrets: you knew death was coming all along.

Fun

Know what you like. Follow what makes you laugh so hard you have to hold your ribs to breathe. It can take a lifetime to sort this out because:

1. It changes as we age.
2. It's hard to separate what we're supposed to like from what we actually enjoy (I like running naked through parks, and I'll burn in hell I'm sure).
3. Other people, especially adults, rarely approve of the good stuff.

Learn to listen to the little voice inside you, the voice of your 8-year-old self, the voice adults (even you) interrupt and speak over, and you'll discover what you love. You might need to take long walks or travel alone, like Buddha, Jesus, and Confucius all did, enjoying stretches where you make every single decision yourself for hundreds of hours, before you'll hear it, but it's there. If you know how to have fun (by yourself, if necessary), you'll always be motivated to do something.

The crazy friend

Cultivate friends who say yes. Yes to midnight road trips. Yes to co-writing bad screenplays. Yes to brainstorming world-domination strategies over lunch. We've all had crazy friends, but after college they fade when careers, families, and other mature pursuits take center stage. Yet when motivation wanes, seek them out.

They're the ones most likely to get what you're talking about and rally around you, increasing the odds you'll get it done. And use the buddy system: be each other's crazy friend.

The discipline

Paul Simon said, "We always have something to say if we're willing to work to find it." Motivations wait inside us, and we can uncover them if we're willing to dig through our fear, sadness, and ambivalence. No professional athlete likes to train every single day, but they do. No professional writer likes to write every single day, but they do, too. The discipline of motivation isn't militarism: don't play drill sergeant (although at times, that might work). Instead, whenever you find yourself unmotivated, run the list of feelings and questions of likely motivations, and see which ones get your heart rate going. Ask yourself: a week from now, will I wish I had worked today or slacked off? It requires discipline to seek motivation when feeling unmotivated, but that's the difference between an artist and someone who fantasizes about being one. And for that purpose, I hope this book has helped you discover what you are capable of.

Research and recommendations

This appendix will fuel the curious: I've provided copious notes for anyone seeking more knowledge about the topics covered throughout this book. There are two bibliographies—one annotated, the other ranked—and a summary of other research used to support my writing. Good luck; let me know what gems you find.

Annotated bibliography

Myths and mythology

There are many types of myths, but in this book I focused on the ones people take to be literal facts, though there is clear evidence to the contrary. Other kinds of myths, such as those found in cultural mythologies (e.g., Greek), are generally not taken literally and serve a different purpose for people who read and enjoy them. I had initially planned to explore such myths in this book as well, but as it developed, the book centered on the pejorative kind. To explore the power of these kinds of myths, here are my two favorite books.

Campbell, Joseph and Bill Moyers. *The Power of Myth*. Anchor, 1991.

> The most accessible book in the Joseph Campbell canon. It's a set of interviews conducted by Bill Moyers that covers many of the major themes in Campbell's other works. Of prime importance is that this text explains why myths matter, how they function, and their relevance to today's challenges. If you like this book, follow up with Campbell's *Myths to Live By* (Souvenir Press Ltd, 1995).

Armstrong, Karen. *A Short History of Myths*. Canongate, 2005.

> This short book follows the history of myths from the beginnings of creation myths to the modern age. Armstrong is a master at approaching the subject of belief in an informal yet scholarly way, and she provides an excellent counterpoint to *The Power of Myth*. Both books avoid getting into pantheons or comparative mythology, but they plant seeds for why you'd want to go there.

Business innovation

Few popular books on business innovation properly credit the earlier works that defined the field. It's common for books to reuse ideas clearly defined and popularized, yet not properly credit them. I find these somewhat older books to be more powerful because they've held up well over years, indicating the authors captured deeper wisdom.

Drucker, Peter. *Innovation and Entrepreneurship.* Collins, 1993.

> A star in my research. His approach is wise and concise, he writes well, and he uses stories more than statistics to support claims. If you want to understand the business of innovation or are interested in startup ventures, this is a must-read.

Hargadon, Andrew. *How Breakthroughs Happen: The Surprising Truth About How Companies Innovate.* Harvard Business School Press, 2003.

> Hargadon touches on many themes found in my research, and he emphasizes interesting stories from history over charts and statistics. My only regret is that I didn't find this book earlier.

Foster, Richard. *Innovation: The Attacker's Advantage.* Simon & Schuster, 1988.

> As best I can tell, this is the first book that uses the S-curve of innovation, a model reused in many modern business books. There's often value in returning to the source of ideas, and Foster does not disappoint. Unlike the two books listed previously, this book is largely about strategy and tactics, but it also provides the reasons, based on history, that those tactics work. *Mastering the Dynamics of Innovation*, by James M. Utterback, is similarly overlooked—it doesn't get much mention today, but deserves it.

Kawasaki, Guy. *The Art of the Start: The Time-Tested, Battle-Hardened Guide for Anyone Starting Anything.* Portfolio, 2004.

> With this title, you know the author knows marketing. This short book is thin on history or theory, but is full of action, motivation, and guts. It's the antidote to the ever-present innovation killer of too much thinking and not enough doing.

Creative thinking and problem solving

I've read classics, bestsellers, research papers, and scientific studies on these subjects. However, the more powerful illustrations of the key ideas come from narratives and first-person accounts of invention. These stories stayed with me longer, had deeper meaning, and simultaneously prove more potent when I've used them in lectures or workshops.

Medina, John. *Brain Rules*. Pear Press, 2008.

> This is the best single account of neuroscience research, including how to make best use of your brain for creativity and everything else. Medina is an excellent writer, in turns entertaining and provocative. Highly recommended.

Csikszentmihalyi, Mihaly. *Creativity: Flow and the Psychology of Discovery and Invention*. HarperPerennial, 1997.

> He's a master of creativity research, and this book is my favorite of his works. It's based on a long-term study of many creative minds, examining their points of view on how creativity happens. His research provided the clearest description of the processes described in Chapter 1.

From the Earth to the Moon, Episode 5: "Spider," HBO, 1998.

> This is part five of an excellent dramatization of NASA's race to the moon. This episode focuses on the design of the lunar lander: a fantastic story of politics, ignored ideas, creative problem solving, collaboration, and dozens of other topics. Highly recommended. Watch it with your coworkers, and compare and contrast to how your organization operates. This is an excellent companion to the film *Apollo 13*.

Brown, Kenneth A. *Inventors at Work: Interviews with 16 Notable American Inventors*. Microsoft Press, 1988.

> This is a series of interviews with great inventors of the 20th century and is a companion to *Programmers at Work*, by Susan M. Lammers, also from Microsoft Press. If you want to innovate, the best bet is to listen to those who do it as they talk about how it's done; this collection hits on many great themes and stories. Forget "how to be creative" books—read these guys and then get to work. (Also see Jessica Livingston's

Founders at Work: Stories of Startups' Early Days [Apress, 2008].)

Stone, Irving. *The Agony and the Ecstasy*. NAL Trade, 2004.

Historical fiction can be tough, but this one gets it right. It's Michelangelo's life written as a novel, but based on extensive research. This book is highly recommended for high-minded innovators. Michelangelo was one of the greats, and the details of his life—especially his resistance to the powers of the day—will put fire in your heart. There is a 1965 film of the same name, but read the book first. The film stars Charlton Heston and doesn't have the same insights for would-be innovators as the book (but it is a fun watch over beers with sarcastic artists and creatives).

Flatow, Ira. *They All Laughed*. HarperCollins, 1992.

This book is a series of short pieces about how many great inventions came to be, including television, Teflon, copy machines, Vaseline, and Silly Putty. Flatow's angle is drama and suffering, as all of these stories are unexpectedly complicated, difficult, and frustrating (for the inventors, not the readers). It's not deep history, and there are some inaccuracies, but it's highly accessible, thought provoking, and humbling.

History and culture

One definition of wisdom is context. You need to be able to compare one thing to another to have insight and act wisely. To master any field, you eventually have to look backward—that's where the clearest picture of what happened and why can be found, yielding context for you in the present. Perhaps one-third of the books I read during research were history books of one kind or another, both to compare accounts of past events and to better understand how to use history as a tool in the present.

Loewen, James W. *Lies My Teacher Told Me*. Touchstone, 1996.
Zinn, Howard. *A People's History of the United States*. HarperCollins, 1980.

It takes courage to surface truths that have been paved over for decades, and both of these books take that challenge head on. Loewen's book, focused on an analysis of American school textbooks, is worth the price for its retelling of Thanksgiving alone. Zinn's work, more politically minded, will close the gap between how Americans see themselves compared to how the world sees them. Both are worldview-shifting books; however, they do sometimes fall into a trap I tried to avoid: telling you what didn't happen, instead of what did.

Carr, Edward Hallett. *What Is History?* Vintage, 1967.

Books that blow your mind in 200 pages deserve special praise; this is one of them. Some others in the field of historiography find this book too dramatic and provocative, but it worked for me, showing me the big questions that historians are supposed to ask and making me interested in the answers.

Pacey, Arnold. *The Maze of Ingenuity.* MIT Press, 1992.

Pacey's aim is to show the parallels between innovation today and Western innovations over the centuries, including an emphasis on how cultures at different times perceived the value of their works. It's a short, dense book, but if you like surprises about how old technologies were made, you'll enjoy and remember it.

Rogers, Everett M. *Diffusion of Innovations.* Free Press, 1995.

As mentioned earlier, this anthropological approach to understanding innovation was compelling and influential. The book is long and academic in style, but the stories are so good that you won't mind. Skipping around is OK because the main points are established early and referenced throughout.

Ranked bibliography

Traditional bibliographies are rarely useful. They obscure the relative value of prior works and ignore how the author used them (were the sources devoured, skimmed, or used as a paperweight?). In addition to the annotated bibliography, I experimented with different formats for a comprehensive listing, and the result is this ranked bibliography. The intention is to indicate which sources drew attention, and how often, during my research.

The order below is based on a review of more than 200 pages of my research notes. Every note I took from a book counted as one point and the references are listed in ranked order. There is no ideal system for ranking influence (the flaw in this one is that not all notes influenced me equally), but this was the best of all those suggested.

82, *Innovation and Entrepreneurship*, Peter Drucker

67, *How Breakthroughs Happen: The Surprising Truth About How Companies Innovate*, Andrew Hargadon

55, *Diffusion of Innovations*, Everett M. Rogers

55, *The Engines of Our Ingenuity*, John H. Lienhard

52, *Creativity in Science: Chance, Logic, Genius, and Zeitgeist*, Dean Keith Simonton

50, *Fire in the Crucible: The Alchemy of Creative Genius*, John Briggs

49, *The Grace of Great Things: Creativity and Innovation*, Robert Grudin

46, *Really Useful: The Origins of Everyday Things*, Joel Levy

46, *Breakthrough: Stories and Strategies of Radical Innovation*, Mark Stefik and Barbara Stefik

44, *Innovation: The Basis of Cultural Change*, H. G. Barnett

36, *The Maze of Ingenuity*, Arnold Pacey

35, *Beethoven: The Universal Composer*, Edmund Morris

34, *Creativity: Beyond the Myth of Genius*, Robert W. Weisberg

33, *The Evolution of Technology*, George Basalla

32, *Mastering the Dynamics of Innovation*, James M. Utterback

30, *Sparks of Genius*, Robert S. Root-Bernstein and Michele M. Root-Bernstein

28, *Connections*, James Burke

27, *What Is History?*, Edward Hallett Carr

26, *The Innovation Paradox: The Success of Failure, the Failure of Success*, Richard Farson and Ralph Keyes

24, *A Brief History of the Future*, John Naughton

23, *The Company: A Short History of a Revolutionary Idea*, John Micklethwait and Adrian Wooldridge

22, *Isaac Newton*, James Gleick

22, "Philosophy of History," Paul Newall (*http://www. galilean-library.org/site/index.php?/page/resources?record=47*)

22, *Innovation: The Attacker's Advantage*, Richard N. Foster

21, *Inventors at Work: Interviews with 16 Notable American Inventors*, Kenneth A. Brown

21, *Applied Imagination*, Alex F. Osborn

20, *Future Hype: The Myths of Technology Change*, Bob Seidensticker

19, *Fumbling the Future: How Xerox Invented, Then Ignored, the First Personal Computer*, Douglas K. Smith and Robert C. Alexander

19, *Medici Effect: What Elephants and Epidemics Can Teach Us About Innovation*, Frans Johansson

18, *How We Got Here: A Slightly Irreverent History of Technology and Markets*, Andy Kessler

17, *They All Laughed*, Ira Flatow

17, *Gutenberg: How One Man Remade the World with Words*, John Man

16, *A Short History of Myths*, Karen Armstrong

16, *The Innovators: The Discoveries, Inventions, and Breakthroughs of Our Time*, John Diebold

16, *The Big Idea*, Steven D. Strauss

16, *Origins of Genius: Darwinian Perspectives on Creativity*, Dean Keith Simonton

16, *The Victorian Internet*, Tom Standage

15, *Innovation: Driving Product, Process, and Market Change*, Edward B. Roberts

14, *Bootstrapping: Douglas Engelbart, Coevolution, and the Origins of Personal Computing*, Thierry Bardini

14, *Myth: A Biography of Belief*, David Leeming

12, *Lucky or Smart*, Bo Peabody

12, *Creativity: Flow and the Psychology of Discovery and Invention*, Mihaly Csikszentmihalyi

12, *The Progress Paradox: How Life Gets Better While People Feel Worse*, Gregg Easterbrook

12, *The Creative Habit: Learn It and Use It for Life*, Twyla Tharp

12, *The Innovator's Solution: Creating and Sustaining Successful Growth*, Clayton M. Christensen

11, *Lost Discoveries*, Dick Teresi

11, *The Art of the Start: The Time-Tested, Battle-Hardened Guide for Anyone Starting Anything*, Guy Kawasaki

11, *Amazon.com: Get Big Fast*, Robert Spector

11, *Eurekas and Euphorias: The Oxford Book of Scientific Anecdotes*, Walter Gratzer

10, *National Geographic Book of Inventions*, Ian Harrison

10, *Blink*, Malcolm Gladwell

10, *Visions of Technology*, Richard Rhodes

10, *The Google Story*, David A. Vise and Mark Malseed

10, *Alexander the Great's Art of Strategy*, Partha Bose

10, *Technological Innovation: A Critical Review of Current Knowledge*, Patrick Kelly and Melvin Kranzberg

9, *Organizing Genius: The Secrets of Creative Collaboration*, Warren Bennis and Patricia Ward Biederman

9, *The Art of Innovation*, Tom Kelley, Jonathan Littman, and Tom Peters

9, *Blockbusters*, Gary S. Lynn

9, *Harvard Business Review on Innovation*, Harvard Business School Press

9, *Managing Creativity and Innovation*, Harvard Business School Press

8, *Ten Theories of Human Nature*, Leslie Stevenson and David L. Haberman

8, *Juice: The Creative Fuel That Drives World-Class Inventors*, Evan I. Schwartz

8, *The Wisdom of Crowds*, James Surowiecki

8, *The Change Function: Why Some Technologies Take Off and Others Crash and Burn*, Pip Coburn

8, *The Act of Creation*, Arthur Koestler

8, *Founders at Work: Stories of Startups' Early Days*, Jessica Livingston

8, *The Sciences of the Artificial*, Herbert A. Simon

7, *Forbes' Greatest Business Stories of All Time*, Daniel Gross

7, *Salt: A World History*, Mark Kurlansky

7, *One Good Turn: A Natural History of the Screwdriver and the Screw*, Witold Rybczynski

6, *Higher: A Historic Race to the Sky and the Making of a City*, Neal Bascomb

6, *We Reach the Moon: The Story of Man's Greatest Adventure*, John Noble Wilford

6, *The Search: How Google and Its Rivals Rewrote the Rules of Business and Transformed Our Culture*, John Battelle

6, *Dealing with Darwin: How Great Companies Innovate at Every Phase of Their Evolution*, Geoffrey A. Moore

6, *Just for Fun: The Story of an Accidental Revolutionary*, Linus Torvalds and David Diamond

6, *Industrial Creativity: The Psychology of the Inventor*, Joseph Rossman

5, "Scientific Method," Wikipedia (*http://en.wikipedia.org/wiki/Scientific_method*)

5, *Innovation: The Missing Dimension*, Richard K. Lester and Michael J. Piore

4, *The Perfect Thing: How the iPod Shuffles Commerce, Culture, and Coolness*, Steven Levy

4, *Invention by Design: How Engineers Get from Thought to Thing*, Henry Petroski

4, *The Private Life of a Masterpiece*, Monica Bohm-Duchen

4, "Johannes Gutenberg," Wikipedia (*http://en.wikipedia.org/wiki/Johannes_Gutenberg*)

4, *The Structure of Scientific Revolutions*, Thomas S. Kuhn

4, *Mavericks: How to Lead Your Staff to Think Like Einstein, Create Like Da Vinci, and Invent Like Edison*, Donald W. Blohowiak

4, *The Eureka Effect: The Art and Logic of Breakthrough Thinking*, David Perkins

3, *Creativity in Business*, Michael Ray and Rochelle Myers

3, *The Map of Innovation: Creating Something Out of Nothing*, Kevin O'Connor and Paul B. Brown

3, *Innovation at the Speed of Laughter: 8 Secrets to World-Class Idea Generation*, John Sweeny

3, *Revolution in Science*, I. Bernard Cohen

2, *Dealers of Lightning: Xerox PARC and the Dawn of the Computer Age*, Michael A. Hiltzik

2, *The Sociology of Invention*, S. C. Gilfillan

1, *The Perfect Store: Inside eBay*, Adam Cohen

1, *The Future of Ideas: The Fate of the Commons in a Connected World*, Lawrence Lessig

1, "Of Innovations," Francis Bacon (*http://oregonstate.edu/instruct/phl302/texts/bacon/bacon_essays.html/*)

1, *Cracking Creativity: The Secrets of Creative Genius*, Michael Michalko

1, *When Old Technologies Were New*, Carolyn Marvin

1, *Mavericks at Work: Why the Most Original Minds in Business Win*, William C. Taylor and Polly LaBarre

0, *The Art of Project Management*, Scott Berkun

Other research sources

- **Interviews.** Over the course of two years, I interviewed more than 100 people, ranging from phone/email conversations to serendipitous airplane and bus chitchat, and all the way to conference-room debates and multihour beer-enhanced discussions. These conversations were a primary source of inspiration for sorting out which myths to cover and the most useful angle of exploration for each one. Interviews are the only way to access true stories of innovation too graphic, embarrassing, absurd, or criminal to ever find their way on the record.

- **Lectures and discussion.** Some of the book's themes were presented in lectures at Google, Microsoft, Amazon.com, Adaptive Path MX, Seattle Mindcamp, O'Reilly's FOO camp and Ignite!, University of Washington, and MIT. I'm grateful for all those who asked questions, pointed out mistakes, and laughed at my jokes.

- **Blog.** As an experiment, I used my website to raise questions, ask for references, propose hypotheses for feedback, and extend the reach of my research. It proved a fantastic way to benefit from people I'd never have had access to otherwise.

- **Survey.** 110 people who identified themselves as innovators filled out an online questionnaire exploring both general innovation and innovation mythology. These people ranked from scientists to writers to computer programmers to artists. This survey was intended to provide anecdotal evidence, and the results are not of a rigor to infer much beyond what was mentioned in Chapter 6. Selections of the results can be found at *http://www.scottberkun.com/blog/?p=422/*.

- **Time.** The paperback edition benefited from nearly three years of visiting corporations, organizations, and start-up companies, further exploring the ideas in the original edition. The ideas in this book have had significant mileage and I'm hopeful they'll stand up long into the future. But if they don't, and they're replaced with better ways to understand, I'll be pleased.

Photo credits

Chapter openers

Preface, New York, NY, U.S., Yann Le Coroller (*http://www.hikari.fr/*)

Chapter 1, Taken at Langeoog, Germany, Lothar Knopp (*http://www.flickr.com/photos/lotse*)

Chapter 2, Paris, France, Frank Lee (*http://www.flee.com*)

Chapter 3, Highway 9 in Santa Cruz, CA, U.S., Chuck Rogers (*http://www.flickr.com/photos/two-wrongs*)

Chapter 4, David's Seattle apartment, David Adam-Edelstein (*http://www.noise-to-signal.com*)

Chapter 5, Melbourne, Australia, James Robertson (*http://www.flickr.com/photos/shingen_au*)

Chapter 6, Melbourne, Australia, James Robertson (*http://www.flickr.com/photos/shingen_au*)

Chapter 7, Lijiang, China, Fillip Forte (*http://flickr.com/photos/fortes/*)

Chapter 8, Taken at Sanssouci, Potsdam, Germany, Lothar Knopp (*http://www.flickr.com/photos/lotse*)

Chapter 9, Texas, U.S., Robin Walker (*http://www.pbase.com/walk1*)

Chapter 10, Langeoog, Germany, Lothar Knopp (*http://www.flickr.com/photos/lotse*)

Chapter 11, San Francisco, CA, U.S., Steve Rotman (*http://www. flickr.com/photos/phunk/25923140/*)

Chapter 12, Phra Nakhon Si Ayutthaya, Thailand, McKay Savage (*http://www.flickr.com/photos/mckaysavage/381693996/*)

Chapter 13, Prague, Czech Republic, Goran Patlejch (*http://www. flickr.com/photos/patlejch/4205226569/*)

Chapter 14, Bilbao, Basque Country, Spain, Joris Verboomen (*http://www.flickr.com/photos/jovivebo/197845214/*)

Appendix, James Hague (*http://www.flickr.com/photos/jhague/ 130509761/*)

Figures

Figure 2-2, Photograph by Maria Kaloudi

Figure 3-1, Photograph by Liam Abrahamsen

Figure 4-1, Photograph by Jimmy Wewer

Figure 8-1, Courtesy NASA/JPL-CalTech

Figure 9-1, © Tate, London, 2007

Figure 10-2, W1950-3-1, Rubens, Peter Paul; *Prometheus Bound;* Philadelphia Museum of Art: Purchased with the W.P. Wilstach Collection, 1950

Figure 10-3, AP/Wide World Photos

Acknowledgments

For the paperback edition

Shouldn't a book on innovation try out some new ideas? Since I was curious—though skeptical—about crowdsourcing (using the Web to let many people contribute to something), I invited readers of *www.scottberkun.com* to volunteer to help with this paperback edition of *The Myths of Innovation*. More than 60 people signed up: some didn't do much, but more than 20 contributed significantly. Some friends helped out, too. We divided up the book into chapters, and individuals signed up to find typos, suggest corrections, improve references, offer counterarguments, and generally help to make this edition as accurate and current as possible. It's a privilege as a writer to get this much help, and I'm grateful.

The team: Divya Manian, Paul Tevis, Vasu Srinivasan, Sara Vermeylen, Nathan Bashaw, Chris Granger, Kimm Viebrock, Bella Martin, Ben Ahroni, Terence Tourangeau, Kav Latiolais, Rob Davis, Harald Felgner, Branimir Ćorluka (we got the Ć right, yes?), Andrew E. McAdams, Allison Jacobsen and Piotr Tyburski (who were my URL Overlords), Dan Roberts, Ian Tyrrell, Simon Rogers, Del Cook, Dmitri Schoeman, Royal Winchester, Jody Rae Prival Myers, and Mike Nitabach.

Thanks to Mary Treseler, Marlowe Shaeffer, Rachel Monaghan, Mark Paglietti, Sara Peyton, and everyone at O'Reilly Media who helped make this paperback edition possible.

Music listened to while working on this edition: Cake, Johnny Cash, Elliott Smith, Cat Power, Pink, National Trust, Caledonia, The Cars, Public Image Ltd, The Clash, Dropkick Murphys, Mozart, Sonny Rollins, Patty Griffin.

For the original edition

To Jill: for 16 years of everything.

Mary O'Brien, my editor, for having the courage to say yes, for earning my trust, and for leaving me alone just enough.

Marlowe Shaeffer, friend and rock-star production editor extraordinaire, and the book team of Kate Basart (cover), Rob Romano (illustrations), Ron Bilodeau (interior design), Caitrin McCullough (editorial), Sara Peyton (PR), Steve Fehler (creative director), Reba Libby (proofreader), and Ellen Troutman (indexer).

The quiet of many 2 a.m. nights, and the crazy owls that kept me company.

Bob Baxley for calling me a coward (he was right). And Christopher Konrad for calling me a MOFO (also right).

All the people who didn't answer my emails and feel bad about it right now.

The Avett brothers for reminding me to go all out—never do anything by half.

To Richard Stoakley, Bob Baxley, and Faisal Jawdat for feedback on the early outline.

The ever-brave chapter review crew: Faisal Jawdat, Robin Jeffries (Google), Bryan Zug, James Refill, and Bob Baxley.

To teachers and mentors: Todd Berkun, Rob Elkins, Jerry Reinstein, Adam Stein, Don Cole, Wilfred Seig, Joe Belfiore, Chris Jones, Steve Capps, and Mark Ashley.

The King County library system and the elves who make interlibrary book loans possible.

For lending me time: Jeff Hawkins, Cory Ondrejka, Ian Phillips, Neil Enns, Stephen Rosenthal, Mark Colburn, Prasadi de Silva, Gary Flake, Derek Bates, John Musser, Richard Stoakley (Overcastmedia.com), Kenneth Norton, Kevin Schofield, Lynn Cherny, Erin

McKean, Greg Linden, Adam Green, Matt Conway, Josh Strater, Brian Hutchinson, Ross Andrus, Mike Vance, Sachin Bhatia, Ian White, Paul Sauruzi, Saul Griffith, Joshua Schauer, Gaurav Oberoi and Chuck Groom (Billmonk.com), Hillel Cooperman (Jacksonfish. com), Piero Sierra, David Hounsell (CMU), John Li (menuism. com), Steve Capps, Sarah Nelson, and Josh Orum (and those names forgotten in the loss of Moleskine #7 on Continental Flight 1739; godspeed, little doodle).

For permissions, advice, blog comments, and other bits of goodness: Mark Denovich, Carrie Devine, Gregory Raiz, James Bullock, Timothy Johnson, Jeff De Cagna, Powel Brodzinksi, Courtney Center, Dan Saffer, Brian Jepson, Jim Kalbach, Kevin Morrill, Rami Nasser, Eric Nehrlick, Peter Cavallo, Hanif Rehman, Catarina Flake, Dion Hinchcliffe, Jay Zipursky, Justin Martinstein, Noah Brier, Konrad West, Alexis Leon, Jason Fried, Bill Stevenson, Rory O'Connor, Gernot D Ross, John Jantos, Sam Greenfield (wiseass), Rob Lefferts, Leddom Lefferts, Shawn Murphy, Phil "5-card stud" Simon, Chris "cycling is not a sport" McGee, Mike "spin-move" Viola, David "pretty boy" Sanberg, Joe "gourmet" Mirza, and the ever-resplendent Richard "Chinaski" Grudman.

Music listened to during the writing of this book: Wonderful Smith, Neutral Milk Hotel, Avett Brothers (constantly), Arcade Fire, Johnny Cash, The Shins, Thelonious Monk, Mozart, Beethoven, Bell X1, Cat Power, Aimee Mann, The Breeders, Belly, Cake, Paul Cantelon, Elliott Smith, The Gossip, Jack Johnson, King Missile, Velvet Underground, Frank Sinatra, The Long Winters, REM, Radiohead, Social Distortion, Woody Guthrie, Bruce Springsteen, Sleater-Kinney, Regina Spektor, and Cut Chemists.

How to help this book:
A request from the author

Thank you for buying this book. If somehow it exceeded your expectations or left you feeling like "gee, things would be better if more people read it," this page is for you.

As you know by now, I'm a young independent author. I don't have a huge marketing machine behind me, nor a gang of billionaire friends, or even a magic genie offering me three wishes. But that's OK. If you're willing to chip in a few minutes of your time, you can seriously help this book find its way in the cold, tough world, where many good books never reach all the people they should.

Please consider any of the following:

- Write a review on Amazon.com.
- Post about this book to your blog, Facebook, or Twitter.
- Recommend the book to coworkers, your friends, and your friends' friends, or even to your friends who blog, or your coworkers' friends who blog, or even your friends of friends who blog about their friends' blogs. The possibilities are endless.
- If you know people who write for newspapers or magazines, drop them a line—or perhaps Oprah or Jon Stewart owes you a favor. If so, now is a good time to cash it in.
- If you like to pretend you're a secret agent, secretly leave a copy of this book on the desk of someone important or influential.

- Go to *www.scottberkun.com* and discover all the great things I write about each week. If you like what you find, run through this list again with that in mind.

These little things make a huge difference. As the author, my opinion of the book carries surprisingly little weight. But you, dear reader, have all the power in the world.

Not only can you help this book find its way, but you'd also make the many risks of writing the next book easier to overcome, increasing the odds I'll do an even better job the next time around.

As always, thanks for your help and support.

—Scott

About the author

Scott Berkun was a manager at Microsoft from 1994–2003, working on projects including v1–5 (not 6) of Internet Explorer. He is the author of three bestselling books, *Making Things Happen*, *The Myths of Innovation* (hardcover), and *Confessions of a Public Speaker* (all published by O'Reilly).

Scott works full-time as a writer and speaker, and his work has appeared in the *New York Times*, *Forbes* magazine, the *Economist*, the *Washington Post*, *Wired* magazine, National Public Radio, and other media. He contributes regularly to *Harvard Business Review* and *BusinessWeek*, has taught creative thinking at the University of Washington, and has appeared as an innovation and management expert on MSNBC and on CNBC. He writes frequently on innovation and creative thinking at his surprisingly popular blog, *www.scottberkun.com*, and on Twitter: @berkun.

His ambition in life is to fill the above bookshelf, which is by his writing desk, with books he has written. If he were smarter, he'd have picked a smaller shelf.

Scott is based in Seattle, WA, but he speaks often around the world about creativity and other topics he's written about. If you'd like to hire him to speak at an event, head over here: *www.scottberkun.com*. You can watch videos of him in action and get in touch.

Index

Numbers

3M, 49

A

accident, invention by, 42
adoption of innovations, 64–67
   analysis of influential
      factors, 117–119
   factors affecting, 65
   forcing, 122
   goodness/adoption
      paradox, 123–126
   metric system, 120
"ahead of its time" label, 64
Aiken, Howard H., 59
airplanes, invention of, 140–142
Amazon.com, 14
anger as motivator, 188
Apollo 13 mission, 38
Apple, 62
   founding of, 44
   framing of Apple IIe
      development
      problems, 133
   precedents to Mac, iPod, and
      iPhone, 73
   release of Apple II
      computer, 31
   VisiCalc spreadsheet, 80
Applied Imagination, 92

apprentices, 78
Archimedes' Eureka, 10
Armstrong, Neil, 76
Art of Innovation, 104
"As We May Think", 13
associative ability, 12
automobiles
   gas-powered, ascendancy of, 29
   good and bad consequences
      of, 147
   innovations that preceded
      Ford, 73
   invention of, 70
   negative reception of Ford's
      first cars, 86

B

Backpack, 133
bad effects of innovations, 143
   acceleration of technology, 150
   automobiles, 147
   DDT, 145, 147
   future and past, 151
bad effects of inventions
   automobiles, PCs, and cell
      phones, 147
banning of literary classics, 54
Basalla, George, 29
beating your competitors, 46
Beethoven, Ludwig von, 89
Bell, Alexander Graham, 54, 61

Berners-Lee, Tim, 6, 123–125
best ideas winning, myth
    of, 112–126
    goodness/adoption
        paradox, 123–126
    secondary factors of
        innovation, 116–119
    space, metrics, and Thomas
        Jefferson, 119–123
    why people believe the best
        wins, 113–116
Beta vs. VHS video, 119
Blockbusters, 133
Bodanis, David, 81
body, using to help your
    mind, 173
Brain Rules, 173, 196
brainstorming
    finding ideas and turning off
        filters, 93
    history and misuse of, 92
    idea finding, 93
brand names, dominant, 72
breaks, importance of, 11
breakthroughs, 12
Bricklin, Dan, 80
Brin, Sergey, 54
Brown, John Seely, 130
Brown, Kenneth A., 196
browser wars, 33
Burke, James, 81
Bush, Vannevar, 13
business innovation, books
    on, 195
business management, 98–109
    challenges of managing
        innovation, 102–109
    environment, 104
    execution, 107
    life of ideas, 103
    persuasion, 108
    protection, 106
    old-school command and
        control attitude, 101
business schools, 101
Butter, Andrea, 133

C

Cage, John, 39
calculus, 75
Campbell-Swinton, A. A., 76
Carlson, Chester, 99
Carr, Edward, 24, 28, 198
Carson, Rachel, 146
cathode ray tubes, 76
Catmull, Ed, 161
cell phones, 13
    good and bad effects of, 147
    history of development, 73
challenges of innovation, 44–47
    acceptance of innovative
        ideas, 59
    honesty about limits of
        knowledge, 162
change, demanded by ideas, 176
Christensen, Clayton M., 62
Chrome browser, 33
collaboration in innovation, 78,
    158
Columbus, Christopher, 23
combination of ideas, 94
combinations, creativity as, 169
comedy, improvisational, classes
    in, 174
commitment, 172
compatibility of innovation to
    current methods, 65
competitors, 46
complexity of innovations, 65
computer mouse, 14
    origins of, 41
    predecessors to Apple
        Macintosh, 73
computer technology, evolution
    of, 26
Connections, 81
Cook, Scott, 130
Cooper, Martin, 73
copy machine, 41, 99
cost vs. relative advantage of
    innovations, 65
Craigslist.org, 49
crazy friends as motivators, 190

crazy necessity as motivator, 189
creative thinking, 168–174
　books on, 196
　combinations, 169
　environment, 171
　inhibition, 170
　killing romance of
　　creativity, 168
　persistence, 172
　tactics for, 173
creativity
　acknowledgment of individual
　　creativity, 77
　creative geniuses, 77
　effects of advancing civilization
　　upon, 85
　Greek goddesses (or muses)
　　representing, 5
　knowing-doing gap, 156
　link to ability to see ideas as
　　fluid and free, 91
　myth of declining ability in
　　adulthood, 84
　origins of, 2
　study of thought processes of
　　creative people, 10
　switching between different
　　projects, 12
Creativity in Science, 75
Creativity: Flow and the
　　Psychology of Discovery
　　and Invention, 10
criticisms of innovative
　　ideas, 57–61
　idea-killing phrases, 90
　innovator's dilemma, 62
　mapping to deeper issues, 59
　negative remarks innovators
　　hear, 86
Csikszentmihalyi, Mihaly, 10, 196
culture, influence on
　　innovation, 117
curiosity, excessive and
　　dreamy, 38
customers, 45
　reaching potential, 46

D

da Vinci, Leonardo, 12, 45
　as creative genius, 77
　frustration with employers and
　　peers, 63
Dark Ages, 28
Davy, Humphrey, 70
DDT, 145–147
　good and bad effects of, 147
de Mestral, George, 42
death as motivator, 190
delivery of ideas, 177
derivatives and CDOs, 149
Dewey, John, 130
Dickens, Brian, 76
difficulty of innovation, 47
Diffusion of Innovations, 64, 198
diffusion of innovations
　metric system, 120
　psychological and sociological
　　factors in, 65
Digital Equipment
　　Corporation, 57
digital music player, 73
discipline of motivation, 191
DNA, 40
doing rather than reading, 174
dominant design, 117
Drew, Richard G., 49
Drucker, Peter, 14, 100, 161, 195
Dyson, Freeman, 11

E

E=mc2, 81
ease of adoption of
　　innovations, 125
eBay Corporation, 6
economics
　influence on adoption of
　　innovation, 118
　Internet use, 125
　subprime crisis of 2007, 149
Edison, Thomas, 42, 70
　framing problem behind
　　lightbulb, 131
　star persona as shield for
　　innovation, 106

Edmonson, Amy C., 102
Eiffel Tower, 57
Einstein, Albert, 52
    defining a problem, 129
    on imagination, 85
    motivation for special theory of
        relativity, 130
    origins of E=mc2, 81
electric light
    inventor of, 70
    problem of precedence, 71
elevator pitch, 181
Emerson, Ralph Waldo, 115, 171
Engelbart, Douglas, 112
Engines of Our Ingenuity, 80
English measurement system, 120
    factors influencing its retention
        in the U.S., 123
entrepreneurship
    arising from frustration plus
        innovation, 62
    knowing-doing gap, 156
    technological innovation
        and, 62
environment for creativity, 171
environment for innovation, 104
    leadership and trust, 164
epiphanies, 2–15
    connections to previous
        ideas, 7–13
    defined, 5
    getting past obsession with, 159
    innovation without, 13–15
    serendipity as example of, 136
Eureka (Archimedes), 10
evolution and innovation, 25–34
    dominant designs dominating
        history, 29–34
    fallacies of evolution, 26–29
Evolution of Technology, 29
evolutionary advantage in fear of
        new things, 55
execution (of ideas), 107
experts on innovation, 156

F

facts, ideas, and solutions, 93
failures
    being happy about interesting
        mistakes, 164
    learning from failure of
        pitches, 184
    rewarding interesting
        failures, 50
Farnsworth, Philo, 76
fears
    advantages of, 55
    interference with
        innovation, 170
    managing fears of
        innovation, 55
Feynman, Richard, 12
Field of Dreams, 115
filters, ideas and, 92–95
    turning off filters, 93
finance, derivatives and
        CDOs, 149
financial obligations, 46
financing your own project, 185
Firefox browser, 33
Flatow, Ira, 197
Flickr, 47
forcing adoption of
        innovations, 122
Ford, Henry, 70, 86
    management philosophy, 100
    precedents in invention of
        automobile, 73
The Fountainhead, 114
Frames of Mind, 84
framing strategy for
        problems, 130–135
    exploring problems with
        prototypes, 135
friends, crazy, as motivators, 190
friendships, powerful, 78
frustration at inability to innovate
        in established
        businesses, 63
Fry, Art, 41
Fuller, Buckminster, 99

fun as motivator, 190
funding innovations, 45

G

Galileo, 54, 60, 129
    failure to pitch his ideas, 176
    importance of time and place of
        birth, 75
Gantt, Laurence, 100
Gardner, Howard, 84
geniuses, 78, 84
Gibson, William, 67
Gladwell, Malcolm, 157
good ideas, 84–95
    dangerous life of ideas, 86
    filters and ideas, 92–95
    how to find, 88–91
goodness
    best ideas winning, myth
        of, 113–116
    focusing on creating good
        products, 163
    goodness/adoption
        paradox, 123–126
    measuring for
        innovations, 140–152
    accelerationn of
        technology, 150
    future and past, 151
    goodness scale, 142–145
    unpredictability of
        innovations, 145–149
    short-term vs. long-term
        thinking, 119
    subjective nature of, 118
Google, 62
    Chrome, 33
    creative workplace, 2
    employees' time for their own
        projects, 48
    environment supportive of
        innovation, 105
    rejection of ideas of
        founders, 54
Gould, Gordon, 9, 148
gravity, discovery of, 4

Greenspan, Alan, 149
Gutenberg, Johannes, 20, 148

H

hard work and persistence, 41,
    155, 172
Hawking, Stephen, 98
Hawkins, Jeff, 132
    prototype design for Palm
        Pilot, 134
Hemingway, Ernest, exploring
        ideas for novels, 89
heroes
    of achievement, 114
    innovators as, 141
    triumph of good, 113
historiography, 24
history and culture,
        bibliography, 197
history of innovation, 18–34
    evolution and
        innovation, 25–34
    honoring the past, 51
    how history changes
        perceptions, 19–21
    myth of the lone
        inventor, 70–81
    why history seems
        perfect, 21–25
history of science, 54
Hoff, Ted, 14, 89
HP, 62
HTML, 116, 123
human shortcomings, 30
humans as pinnacle of
        evolution, 26
hypertext, 112

I

IBM PC, 31
idea journal, 173
ideas, 93
    best ideas win, myth
        of, 112–126
    as combination of other
        ideas, 168

ideas (*continued*)
   combinations of, 7
   difficulty of finding good ideas,
      myth of, 84–95
      ideas and filters, 92–95
      killers of ideas, 90
   elaboration into function, 13
   execution of, 107
   finding, 45
   life of, 103
   love of new ideas, myth
      of, 54–67
      ideas ahead of their
         time, 64–67
   as magic, 3–7
   pitching, 176–185
   switching mode of
      expression, 174
idle time, importance for
      creativity, 11
imagination, 85
improvement, perception of, 28
improvisational comedy class, 174
inevitability of progress, 28
inheritance and tradition, 118
inhibition, 170
Innovation and
      Entrepreneurship, 14,
      161, 195
innovations
   defined, xvi
   finding paths of, 50
   how they start, 38–40
      curiosity, 42
      desire for wealth and
         money, 42
      necessity, 43
      seeds of innovation, 40
   infinite paths of, 47, 47–52
   managing fears of, 55
   secondary factors of, 116–123
Innovator's Dilemma, 62
innovator's dilemma, 61
innovators as American heroes, 73
insight, 12
   observation as key, 12
instant messages, 150

intensity and willingness to
      reconsider
      assumptions, 51
Internet Explorer, 33
Internet, good and bad effects
      of, 150
Intuit, 130
invention, simultaneous, 74–79
Inventors at Work, 196
inversion, 173
iPhone, 73
iPod, 73
Ireland, Great Potato Famine, 150
issues underlying criticism of new
      ideas, 59

J

JavaScript, 116
Jefferson, Thomas, 121
Jobs, Steve, 44, 107

K

Kawasaki, Guy, 79, 195
Kay, Alan, 104, 112
Kelly, Tom, 104
keyboards, QWERTY model, 116,
      117
The Knowing-Doing Gap, 156

L

laptops, 106
laser, invention of, 9, 148
Lauterbur, Paul C., 54
leadership, 161
   importance of, 163
learning required to apply
      innovations, 65
Leibniz, Friedrich, 75
Lienhard, John H., 80, 115
Lies My Teacher Told Me, 23, 197
life of ideas, 103
lightbulb
   convenience of lone
      inventors, 72
   Edison's problem-framing
      strategy, 131
   invention of, 70

Linux, 42
literary classics, rejection of, 54
Lives of a Cell, 105
Loewen, James W., 23, 197
lone inventor, myth of, 70–81
    challenge of simultaneous
            invention, 74–79
    convenience of lone
            inventors, 72
    origins of spreadsheets and
            E=mc2, 79–81
long-term vs. short-term
            thinking, 119
Lost Discoveries, 46
love of new ideas, myth of, 54–67
    entrepreneurship and
            innovation, 62–64
    how innovations gain
            adoption, 64
    innovator's dilemma, 61, 62
    negative remarks made to
            innovators, 57–61
    truth about ideas before their
            time, 64–67
luck, 39
    honoring, 51
Lynn, Gary S., 133

M

Machiavelli, Niccolo, 56
Macintosh computer, 73
    development of, 108
Maes, Pattie, 90
managers, innovation and, 98–109
    challenges of managing
            innovation, 102–109
    conflicts of management and
            innovators, 101
    myth that managers know what
            to do, 98
    risk aversion, 158
    why they fail at innovation, 99
marketing campaigns to promote
            innovations, 72
Mars *Orbiter*, 119
masking tape, invention of, 49

*Mastering the Dynamics of
        Innovation*, 29
The Maze of Ingenuity, 77, 198
McDonald's, 43
Medina, John, 173, 196
meritocracy, 113
method, defined, 37
methodology, 36–38
    how innovations start, 38, 40
    myth of, 37
metric system, 118, 120–123
    factors affecting failure to adopt
            in U.S., 123
    Mars *Orbiter* failure and, 120
    proposal by Thomas Jefferson
            for adoption, 121
Michelangelo
    as creative genius, 78
    frustration with employers and
            peers, 63
    novel about his life, 197
microprocessor, 89
    invention of, 14
Microsoft, 62
Microsoft Internet Explorer, 33
microwave oven, invention of, 136
mind, help from the body, 173
Minnesota Mining and
            Manufacturing Co.
            (3M), 49
MIT Media Lab, 90, 99
Mizoguchi, Tetsuya, 106
modes of expressing ideas,
            switching, 174
money and wealth as motivators in
            innovation, 42
Morse, Samuel, 61
Mosaic web browser, 14, 32
motivation, retaining, 188–191
    listing of important
            motivations, 188–191
Motorola, cell phone
            prototype, 73
Mozilla Firefox, 33
MRI, 54
multiples (simultaneous
            inventions), 75

muses of creativity, 5
  losing the muse, 11
music player (digital), 73
Mystery of Picasso, 89
myths and mythology, 194

N

names of innovations, 72
NASA
  effort to put a person on the
    moon, 76
  failure of Mars *Orbiter*, 119
natural selection, 27
NCSA's Mosaic web browser, 32
necessity, 43
  crazy necessity as
    motivator, 189
  as motivator, 188
Negroponte, Nicholas, 99
Nelson, Ted, 112
Netscape Navigator, 33
Netscape web browser, 14
network, origins of term, 81
new ideas, 55
Newmark, Craig, 49
  founding of Craigslist.org, 43
Newton, Isaac, 4, 51, 128
  invention of calculus, 75
NIH (Not Invented Here)
    syndrome, 94
Nintendo, 73
Nipkow, Paul, 76
The No Asshole Rule, 162
Nobel, Alfred, 114

O

objective history, 24
observability of results of
    innovation, 66
observation as key to insight, 12
Occam's razor, 158
Olsen, Ken, 57
Osborn, Alex F., 92
Outliers, 157

P

Pacey, Arnold, 77, 198
Page, Larry, 54
Palm Pilot, 132
  prototype for, 134
partnerships
  finding a partner for a
    project, 174
  in innovation, 78
patents, 79
paths of innovation, 47–52
  finding, 50–52
Pauling, Linus, 88
PCs (personal computers)
  best ideas win, 112
  good and bad effects of, 147
  history of development, 30–34
  spreadsheets as first killer
    app, 80
Peabody, Bo, 39, 57
*A People's History of the United
    States*, 23, 197
persistence, importance of, 41, 172
personal digital assistants
    (PDAs), 131
perspective of your listener,
    imagining, 180
persuasion, importance of, 108
Pfeffer, Jeffrey, 156
philosopher's stone, 128
photocopier, 41
photo-sharing service (Flickr), 48
physical activity to aid the
    mind, 173
Picasso, Pablo, 12, 89, 135
Piloting Palm, 133
pitching an idea, 176–185
  all ideas demand change, 176
  delivering the pitch, 183
  finding people with power, 179
  going your own way, 185
  imagining perspective of your
    listener, 180
  learning from failure, 184
  making three versions of your
    pitch, 181
  refining your idea, 177

shaping your pitch, 178
testing the pitch, 182
Pixar, 161
play, connection to finding good
        ideas, 91
Pogue, David, 133
political capital for
        innovations, 106
politics, influence on adoption of
        innovations, 118
Post-it Notes, 41
potato famine in Ireland, 150
potential customers, 46
power, 99
    pitching your idea to people
        with power, 179
powerful friendships, 78
precedence, problem of, 71
prerequisite knowledge for
        innovations, 74
pride as motivator, 189
printing press, 20
probability of innovation, 47
problem solving, books on, 196
problems, 128–137
    analyzing problem solved by
        your innovation, 178
    coming up with problem to
        solve, 10
    created by innovation, 144
    framing to help solve
        them, 130–135
        exploring with
            prototypes, 134
    role of serendipity in
        solving, 135–137
problems as invitations, 129
progress, myth of inevitability, 28
Prometheus myth, 141
protection for innovation, 106
prototypes, exploring problems
        with, 134

Q

Quicken and QuickBooks
        software, 130
QWERTY keyboard, 116, 117

R

Rand, Ayn, 114
ranked bibliography, 198–203
reading instead of doing, 174
refining your idea, 177
    basic questions to answer, 178
reification, 159
rejections, preparing for, 176
relative advantage of
        innovations, 65
relaxing events, 56
religions, view of creativity in, 5
reproduction, 45
research sources, 203
resources for innovation, 106
risks of innovation, 37
    allowing others to take, 55
    aversion to risk of
        managers/leaders, 158
    conflict with desire for relaxing
        events, 56
    entrepreneurs vs. large
        organizations, 63
    search for good ideas, 88
    speeding up innovation, 120
rivalries, 78
Rogers, Everett M., 64, 198
Rollins, Henry, 190
Roman architecture, 21
Rosetta Stone, 18
    discovery and translation of, 19
Rosing, Boris, 76
Rules for Revolutionaries, 79

S

schnapps, 74
scope of your idea, assessing, 178
search engines, 14, 73
    rejection of page rank ideas, 54
seeds of innovation, 40
self-contained innovations, 79
self-knowledge, 50, 171
serendipity, 135–137
Shakespeare, William, 170
Sholes, Christopher, 117
short-term vs. long-term
        thinking, 119
significant positive change, xvii

Silent Spring, 146
Simon, Paul, 191
Simonton, Dean, 75
simple plan, 163–165
simultaneous invention, 74–79
size of innovation opportunity, 51
solutions, 93
    finding, 45
    framing problems to aid in
            solution, 130–135
    in search of problems, 148
    truth about
            serendipity, 135–137
Sony Walkman, 73
Spencer, Percy, 135
sponsorship and funding for
            innovations, 45
spreadsheet, origins of, 80
SRI systems, 73
Star Trek (television program), 13
stepping-stones to innovations, 79
stressful events, 55
subconscious
    role in creative thinking, 11
    surfacing of ideas, 173
subprime crisis of 2007, 149
Sutton, Robert I., 156, 162
Swan, Joseph, 70

T

talent
    associative ability, 12
    creative geniuses and, 78
    relationship to environment, 98
Taylor, Frederick, 100
teams
    problems with, 158
    reducing size of, 164
    role of collaboration in problem
            solving, 161
    talented people who don't work
            well on, 162
techno-evolutionism, 26

technological evolution, 26
    acceleration without
            discrimination, 150
    demystified, 27
    dominant designs dominating
            history, 29–34
    entrepreneurship and, 63
    myth of inevitability of past
            innovations, 26
telegraph, invention of, 61
telephone, invention of, 54
television
    high-resolution, 150
    simultaneous inventions, 76
Teresi, Dick, 46
Tesla, Nikola, 78, 131, 141, 155
    technology and weaponry, 141
They All Laughed, 197
Thomas, Lewis, 105, 170
time
    necessary to become good at
            something, 157
    short-term vs. long-term
            thinking, 119
timeliness, ideas ahead of their
            time, truth about, 64–67
timing, challenge of, 46
Torvalds, Linus, 42
Toshiba, 106
Tower of Babel, 142
tradition
    effects on adoption of
            innovation, 118
    innovation and, 152
trialability of innovations, 66
triggers for breakthroughs, 12
Tripod (website), 39
trust, 158
    importance of, 163
    necessity for good
            communication, 160
    placing above any team
            member's abilities, 162

U

U.S. Library of Congress, on
        invention of
        automobiles, 70
unintended consequences of
        innovations, 147, 148, 150
unpredictability of
        innovations, 145–149
Utterback, James, 29

V

value of innovation vs. old
        ways, 65
Velcro, 42
video games, 73
VisiCalc (spreadsheet), 80, 94

W

WD-40, 89
wealth and money as motivators in
        innovation, 42
web browsers, 14
    history of development, 32
websites, 115
    increases in numbers of, 124
Western Union, 61
Westinghouse, George, 155
What Is History?, 24, 198
"What Is This?" game, 95
WHO (World Health
        Organization), 145
willpower and commitment, 172
Windows operating system, 32
wishful thinking as distraction, 155
working environment, 104
World Health Organization
        (WHO), 145
World Wide Web, 14
    factors affecting adoption
        of, 123–126
    invention of, 6
Wright, Orville and Wilbur, 140.

X

Xerox PARC
    development of PC, 31, 73
    environment for
        innovation, 104

Y

Yahoo!, 62

Z

Zinn, Howard, 23, 197
Zworkin, Vladimir, 76

Colophon

The cover and heading font is BentonSans. The text font is Sabon.

Page numbers were hand-carved, based on a Dutch interpretation of a sketch of reproductions of a famous 13th-century Chinese monograph series believed to have been glanced at once by Marco Polo's best friend's sister. Note the glory of the sans-serifed ascenders! They cost extra, you know.

Certain complex interior layout was performed remotely from onboard the International Space Station using—according to the police report—laser beams, an unidentified space gas, and a case of Russian beer.

The ink that makes up these very words was extracted from thousands of adolescent Malaysian juniper beetles, hand-picked for their deep black hues. Blended with tonic water from the Bavarian Alps (northern, not that southern swill), this priceless ink is then stored in the finest French hardwood kegs, which are wrapped in a layer of Egyptian velvet and left to age for centuries while a secret tribe of the world's finest chorally trained children bless them with chants of salvation for all those who read words in colophons written in this ink.

This book, except for ink, fonts, and page numbers, is made from 99% recycled Grade A truffle compost, approved by the International Order of Colophon Authors (IOCA). The remaining 1% was, tragically, only semi-recycled truffle compost that did not meet final level-3 IOCA approval. I am as devastated as you.

I'd like to interrupt this colophon to apologize for our inability to provide the high quality of colophon you have come to expect from O'Reilly. Please believe that we did everything to prevent this from happening. Several recommended colophonists were hired, found unworthy, replaced, fired, shoved (en masse, out of spite), scantily clad, into cold, dark corners and made to read *War and Peace*, in Russian, backward, until finally, at great expense, this colophonist was rightfully chosen to free the imprisoned practitioners of colophon arts and save the day.

Before you go, know that I, anonymous colophon writer, have spared the human race from certain extinction dozens of times through use of my varied colophonic powers. Out of respect, you should always read colophons—you never know what you might find.

Related Titles from O'Reilly

Technology and Society

Confessions of a Public Speaker

Devices of the Soul

Intellectual Property and Open Source

Just a Geek

Open Government

Open Sources

Open Sources 2.0

Revolution in the Valley

Spam Kings

Subject to Change: Creating Great Products & Services for an Uncertain World

The Cathedral & the Bazaar

The Geek Atlas

The Myths of Innovation

The New How

We the Media

Web 2.0: A Strategy Guide

Get even more for your money.

Join the O'Reilly Community, and register the O'Reilly books you own. It's free, and you'll get:

- 40% upgrade offer on O'Reilly books
- Membership discounts on books and events
- Free lifetime updates to electronic formats of books
- Multiple ebook formats, DRM FREE
- Participation in the O'Reilly community
- Newsletters
- Account management
- 100% Satisfaction Guarantee

Registering your books is easy:
1. Go to: oreilly.com/go/register
2. Create an O'Reilly login.
3. Provide your address.
4. Register your books.

Note: English-language books only

To order books online:
oreilly.com/order_new

For questions about products or an order:
orders@oreilly.com

To sign up to get topic-specific email announcements and/or news about upcoming books, conferences, special offers, and new technologies:
elists@oreilly.com

For technical questions about book content:
booktech@oreilly.com

To submit new book proposals to our editors:
proposals@oreilly.com

Many O'Reilly books are available in PDF and several ebook formats. For more information:
oreilly.com/ebooks

O'REILLY®

Spreading the knowledge of innovators   oreilly.com